THE
MICROCOMPUTER
FACILITY AND THE
SCHOOL LIBRARY
MEDIA SPECIALIST

Edited by
E. Blanche Woolls and
David V. Loertscher

American Library Association
Chicago and London 1986

Designed by Deborah Doering

Composed by Precision Typographers
in Times Roman and Avant
Garde on a Quadex/Compugraphic
8400 typesetting system

Printed on 50-pound Glatfelter, a
pH-neutral stock, and bound
in 10-point Carolina cover stock
by Edwards Brothers, Inc.

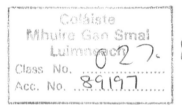
Library of Congress Cataloging-in-Publication Data
Main entry under title:
The Microcomputer facility and the school library media
 specialist.

   1. School libraries—Automation.   2. Instructional
materials centers—Automation.   3. Microcomputers—
Library applications.   4. Media programs (Education)—
Automation.   I. Woolls, E. Blanche.   II. Loertscher,
David V., 1940–
Z675.S3M334   1986   027.8'0285   85-26827
ISBN 0-8389-3325-4

Contents

Introduction

The technological developments which made computing power available to business and home at a reasonable price are allowing all elementary and secondary schools to enter the world of high technology. School library media specialists who are already responsible for technology literacy (use of equipment) and information literacy (access to information in a wide variety of formats and from a wide variety of sources beyond the single school library media center) suddenly are able to offer computer literacy for patrons through the provision of many new and different computer applications. Since the microcomputer is another form of educational technology, the school library media specialist should be a key person in promoting the use of high technology, its products and potential, with teachers and students.

The addition of the microcomputer to the existing technologies in the school library media center provides an opportunity to combine ''concrete'' information with ''fluid'' information. Concrete information includes printed books and magazines, films and filmstrips. Fluid information is information which is ever changing. The live television program, the ''skeleton'' microcomputer program, and the microcomputer as terminal access to a database are examples of fluid information. The opportunities offered through this new technology will help the school library media specialist provide both concrete and fluid information from the widest possible media base and will permit teachers to add exciting and relevant activities to their present curriculum units.

It is appropriate for leadership in microcomputer programs to come from library media specialists for several reasons:

1. The microcomputer has instructional applications across disciplines; library media specialists are accustomed to facilitating interdisciplinary activities from their unique vantage point in the school.

2. The microcomputer is yet another tool for teaching; library media specialists are routinely viewed as providers of instructional tools and materials.
3. Selection of microcomputer software is a critical aspect of the use of this technology in instruction. The library media specialist is the educational professional with the most training in selection of reference and research materials to expand the curriculum beyond the textbook.
4. Providing teacher inservice training on the use of technology in instruction has been a typical expectation for library media specialists.

This book is designed to assist school library media specialists in initiating, maintaining, and expanding microcomputer use in elementary and secondary schools. The contributions of this book were written especially for it and were organized by the order of steps from the planning stages through implementation of program. The first part, Planning the Facility, describes the means for establishing objectives and determining the scope of microcomputer applications. Selecting software is followed by selecting hardware to run the software, and then the facility is set up and prepared for operation. Finally, there's a review of what the research says about computer-assisted instruction and the implications for using microcomputers.

Part 2 is an overview of the operation of the facility as a part of the school library media program. Included are the administrative uses of microcomputers, creating library media management software inhouse, and methods for descriptive cataloging of microcomputer software. The part concludes with a discussion of the use of electronic mail.

Part 3 describes the services available, including dial-up services for students, interactive video, and computer literacy courses.

The final part gives examples of the school library media specialist working with the faculty. A taxonomy for teachers is presented, followed by suggestions for training staff and teachers in the use of the microcomputer. A method for developing a district training plan is followed by one for working with teachers in individual subject disciplines and specialized curricular applications. The book concludes with an example of the implementation of a microcomputer program in a single school.

PART ONE

PLANNING THE FACILITY

Most readers would agree that children are living in an electronic age. If this is not to become a country with a computer elite society, it is essential that children early in their education be provided with appropriate computer experiences in their school and thus become computer literate. The new technology, specifically the microcomputer, provides the introduction to computer literacy and presents one of the greatest challenges for school library media specialists in more than two decades. Not since the influx of federal funds for the purchase of media (NDEA Title III in 1957 followed by ESEA Title II in 1965) has a greater opportunity been given to school library media specialists and other educators. It is indeed fortunate that this innovation, which holds so much promise for teaching children, has implications that apply directly to the media center. While other technologies have had teaching applications for the library media specialist, the microcomputer may be used for reference functions as well as for management of the library media center.

Many school library media specialists experienced major changes with technology in the fifties and sixties. NDEA funds became available to purchase a wide variety of audiovisual equipment and media to expand the use of technology in schools. The allocation and distribution of ESEA Title II in 1965, which provided funds specifically for the purchase of books and media for the library, encouraged the creation of new centers and the expansion of existing school libraries into media facilities. In most elementary schools, media centers came into

1

existence while high school libraries were transformed into media centers as audiovisual materials and equipment joined the existing book collections.

Staff were added to library media centers to help teachers incorporate audiovisual material into their lesson plans and to assist students in the use of media in the media center throughout the school day. Different roles were given to personnel who formerly used only the typewriter and now had to teach how to operate the equipment, manage its distribution and maintenance, and even operate equipment for teachers and students. School library media personnel met the technology challenge in the 1960s and are moving quickly into high technology today.

Microcomputers have been available in schools for half a decade. They have joined other educational innovations which have, at least temporarily, revolutionized teaching and learning. This new tool has come about so rapidly that many school personnel have had little or no time to prepare for it. But, as the initial years of use pass, questions emerge. What is the true role of the microcomputer as an instructional tool? Where in the school should microcomputers be placed? Who in the school should supervise and promote educational computing? It is the premise of this book that microcomputers, as a form of educational technology, can best be placed in the school library media center.

The library media center provides the ideal central organization within the school for a coordinated effort for computer literacy. Since the media center is not a part of any subject department in the school, it is politically neutral. Thus, the media specialist is able to encourage the use of microcomputers throughout the curriculum. Another advantage is that the library media center provides the ideal place where many technologies can be merged together as curricular needs arise.

When microcomputers move into library media centers, some changes occur. Just as staff were added to school library media centers in the 1960s to assure that media were carefully selected and effectively used by students and teachers, additional staff may be needed to assist with the microcomputer program. Certainly the library media center staff and the teachers in their schools will be defining and helping implement ''computer literacy'' in relation to the microcomputer program.

Computer literacy has become a subject of concern to and controversy for school directors, administrators, and teachers who feel the pressure to introduce computers into the school curriculum. Just how to make this introduction has become an argument between advocates of a wide variety of definitions of *computer literacy.*

In order to plan a computer literacy program, a working definition of the term *computer literacy* must be forged. Literacy has meant the ability to read and write. With the advent of high technology, the term has taken a more generic meaning. *Literate* is now defined in *Webster's Ninth New Collegiate Dictionary* as "having knowledge or competence (computer-literate)." Many persons consider computer literacy courses as those which teach about computers, while others feel they are literate if they teach with computers. Computer literacy for some is knowledge of one or more computer languages. For others, it is understanding the history of the development of the computer; for still others, it is the ability to use a computer for one or more activities which the user wishes to have happen. Some persons wish only to use commercially available microcomputer programs, while others wish to develop or modify these programs. Many teachers lack the programming expertise or the time to do either.

As the technology expands, school administrators and media specialists may be forced to answer the question "Should a programmer be hired for the library media center staff?" or "Should the school library media specialist become a programmer?" If the answer to the first question is "Yes," the media specialist will be involved in writing the job description so that the person to be hired can meet the needs of an education community. When hired, the library media specialist will need to make teachers aware of the opportunity and capability such a person offers. This new specialist should be able to assist with software development and with planning for the use of microcomputers in the classroom as well as to expand computer literacy training.

It seems more likely that the second question will receive the affirmative response. Financial constraints may make the addition of specialized staff a remote possibility in most school districts. Rather, a school library media specialist may become the computer expert, the literacy trainer for the school, and even the software program modifier. Additional training must be acquired, and the library media specialist's job description will again be modified. The school library media specialist who adds responsibility for this new technology to the list of other services will find it professionally rewarding. In order to share this excellent resource with the entire school, the school library media specialist must take the responsibility for seeing that all teachers and students have an opportunity to become computer literate.

Perhaps the first assistance the school library media specialist may offer students and teachers is to provide open access to this new technology and a basic introduction to its uses. A second method of helping students, particularly at the elementary level, may be to assist them in learning keyboarding.

Typewriting is taught at the secondary level. It includes formatting as well as recording through keystrokes (keyboarding). Offered in the business department, the class is usually directed to the student who wishes to learn ''formal'' typewriting—skills beyond the needs of those who wish only to use the microcomputer. Since this course is not chosen by all secondary students, some may have no opportunity to learn any keyboarding skills. Students who are not taught correct keyboarding will be forever using less efficient ''hunt and peck'' systems.

Two problems hinder the teaching of keyboarding to young children. The first is the lack of a teacher and the second may be the size of the microcomputer keyboard in relation to the finger reach of 5- and 6-year-olds. The first problem may be overcome if school library media specialists are willing to use a typewriting textbook and teach the basics. Supplemented by microcomputer keyboarding programs, practice in the library media center may become a part of learning the alphabet for kindergarten and first grade students. The second problem may be overcome by the selection of microcomputers with smaller keyboards for teaching keyboarding to these very young children.

Students may also begin learning keyboarding on cardboard simulated keyboards. One teacher was very successful in teaching keyboarding by placing the letters and numbers each finger types on the child's finger. The child may then look at the letter on the finger before striking the key on the simulated keyboard or on the microcomputer itself. Several programs are available for the elementary as well as the secondary student and even for teachers who have never learned to type.

Many opportunities are available to school library media specialists. However, the most efficient and educationally sound use of microcomputers will occur when thorough planning takes place. Program goals and objectives must be developed; available resources must be evaluated and those needed to complete the program must be identified. A systematic plan to reach the goals must be developed, a time-line established so that facilities become operational when scheduled, and processes for anticipated equipment failure established so that the facility remains operational at all times.

School library media specialists who seek and accept the responsibility for management of the microcomputer program for their schools must approach this opportunity from four directions, whether the school district is large or small. They must be concerned about the availability of software, the selection of hardware, the placement or movement of the microcomputer into classrooms, laboratory, or media center, and the maintenance of the system. One more issue remains: the need to maximize both the efficient use of district resources and the effective use of technology.

Part 1 takes the library media specialist through the steps of planning for microcomputer use. Since there is greater complexity in coordinating the activities of a large school district, planning principles are discussed in this context. These principles may be applied in a single school. In the described planning process, program objectives are established; the software which will meet these objectives is then identified. Choosing the hardware is followed by a section on setting up the facility. This part concludes with an article reinforcing the concept of microcomputers centrally located in the school library media center.

Microcomputers in a Large School District

Judy G. Mizik

Microcomputers can suddenly "just appear" throughout a large school district. A parent-teacher organization may sell candy and use the profits to buy a microcomputer or two, or a nearby university may develop a project where local teachers and students at a selected school receive both training and microcomputers. The coordinator of the gifted program may purchase enough microcomputers to establish small laboratories in various schools. A district administrator, a teacher, or a library media specialist may write a proposal and be granted money to purchase microcomputers. A principal may secure funds to establish a small microcomputer classroom. All of these efforts may be concurrent with computer work by the mathematics and computer science departments. Although these endeavors are well intended, the result is a district which has several clusters of different microcomputers and, ultimately, unnecessary duplication of costs due to lack of compatibility. To achieve microcomputer integration within a district, so that students are served by the most cost-effective means, the following is a suggested implementation plan for a large district.

If microcomputers are going to make an impact in any school district, careful planning must precede wide adoption and implementation of this technology. The amount of funds which will be assigned to the purchase of microcomputers will be determined, and the numbers which can be allocated to schools will be decided. Since directors of school library media programs have worked with a variety of funding sources, it may mean that they will have the responsibility for locating additional funding. It may appear that a variety of funding sources are available to large school districts to help their personnel initiate and support the implementation of a new technology. The administration of a large district, with its large total budget, may be able to divert funds for implementation of special programs, but it

7

must also provide for more schools and more students than a small district. All school library media specialists whether in large or small districts should be aware of some of the alternative sources of funding.

Alternative funding possibilities for media specialists with insufficient or, perhaps, nonexistent district budget allotments include block grant funds, government and foundation grants, and grants from microcomputer manufacturers. Local school and community fund raisers are in order for those small districts where one or two microcomputers and some peripheral equipment may meet the initial needs of both the students and library media staff. In some areas shared projects with other agencies, such as the local public library, may increase the availability of microcomputers and microcomputer programs at both locations.

Not only can school library media specialists assume a leadership role in securing funding, but district media personnel must also take a leadership position in the planning process. This may mean helping with the district plan by serving on various committees and subcommittees.

Although microcomputers have been appearing in schools and school library media centers for several years, implementation plans (or ''What do we do with it now?'' decisions) were generally made after the microcomputers had arrived. The literature reveals the disappointments which often followed. Successful district-wide microcomputer program implementation in school library media centers can be attained if educators follow the same practices or prescriptions which are applied with *any* instructional innovation.

Use a systems design approach during the entire microcomputer program development stages. Examine the current research on innovation and planned change strategies to develop a needs assessment document (or documents). Goals and objectives are based upon the results of the needs assessment. Detailed plans are formulated, and the program is put into effect. Program evaluation principles are applied throughout the implementation process, and at the conclusion to assess the degree of success. Clear lines of communication must be maintained at all times.

The product of the goals and objectives stage is the development of a long-range plan which will meet the needs which were identified. When a district makes a commitment to integrate microcomputers with the instructional program, the comprehensive long-range plan should assure that all students receive a computer education appropriate to their ability. The plan may range anywhere from three to seven years. Longer plans may never reach implementation.

District-Level Computer Committee

In a very large school district, with many buildings and students, the long-range plan should be developed by an established district-level computer committee composed of administrative division heads, such as the district library services director, department heads, and building-level school library media specialists. Remember that the committee members will be educators, and do not have to be computer experts. Their commitment to provide the best education possible to students, coupled with their experience and educational expertise, will enable them to "learn computers" as they undertake such a charge. If the budget permits, a position should be opened for a director whose sole charge is to coordinate all of the district's computer endeavors throughout the implementation plan and thereafter. The creation of such a position is imperative particularly in very large districts, which this implementation prescription addresses.

The plan must reflect the needs of the district as elicited from a district-wide computer needs assessment. Examine the status quo in relation to what is desired regarding microcomputers in the district and establish priorities. Goal statements can then be formulated. A minimal number of goals is recommended, broad enough in scope to allow for the inclusion of any existing computer curriculum offerings (such as data processing or computer science courses), as well as all other subject areas. Common goals among districts are to develop and implement a computer literacy program for all students and to integrate computers with the curricula through computer-assisted instruction. The committee's philosophy, anticipated cost factors, and a general timeline are also necessary in the plan.

After it passes through its definition or initiation stage, the committee must seek support of the plan. Approval by the school board and, ideally, a specified budget allotment provide the needed support for the committee to progress. With the long-range plan in hand, the committee must continue to make haste, but slowly. Establish a regular meeting day and time (weekly, if possible). Maintain meeting minutes for a record, and for distribution to those who were absent, and begin to organize the management of the tasks ahead.

The district-level computer committee can now determine various subcommittees, with each district committee member serving as a subcommittee chairperson. These subcommittees will expand the activities outlined in the long-range plan in order to meet specific objectives. Keep in mind that the computer committee represents people who have varying levels of computer knowledge and a myriad of other responsibilities associated with their positions. They can serve as a liaison and clearinghouse to all of the subcommittees. The number and names of the subcommittees will depend upon the long-range goals and the size of the district. In any case, the following areas should be addressed:

1. Existing curriculum and computer integration
2. Computer career education
3. Computer literacy
4. Inservice training

5. Hardware
6. Software
7. Related technologies (e.g., video)
8. Physical location

Subcommittees

Membership for the subcommittees can be drawn from interested school personnel—principals, supervisors, teachers, and, most importantly, school library media specialists. Voluntary participation recruits those who are truly interested and/or talented, and quickly weeds out individuals who are simply seeking extra hours of workshop pay. The number of members per subcommittee will depend upon the committee's charge. A software committee, reviewing materials from several vendors for all of the curriculum areas, may require many more people than the committee that determines the physical location of each microcomputer in each school. School library media specialists should serve on all of the subcommittees to reinforce integration of the library program with the entire curriculum and to determine the library media center's microcomputer utilization.

Subcommittees can meet simultaneously with their particular chairpersons—who keep their members informed of all the other subcommittees' progress—as needed for their work. The chairperson also relates any subcommittee's questions or concerns to the district-level committee which may require that committee's action, permission, or help. The subcommittees must define their mission, prepare a list of enabling objectives to accomplish their mission, and establish a timeline spanning a one-year period. The one-year timeline is advised for the subcommittees so that the deadlines are met, the objectives are accomplished, the members' interest and enthusiasm do not wane, and so that each subcommittee's mission statement can be revised at the end of that period (if necessary).

Plan of Action

The direction first planned by a subcommittee to accomplish its mission may be significantly altered by a number of variables, such as changes in committee membership, failure to meet, failure of some administrators or teachers to follow district guidelines, purchases by parent groups, and so on. These variables may occur during the first year and have an effect upon the implementation plan. When an activity is to be implemented, a subcommittee should have a plan of action which will be coordinated with the plans of other subcommittees. Following is an example of a subcommittee's possible plan of action.

Mission Statement—Physical Location Subcommittee

The Physical Location Subcommittee will develop the criteria to be followed in determining the specific locations of microcomputers within each school.

Timeline: Physical Location Subcommittee

(19–)

Activity	Sept.	Oct.	Nov.	Dec.	Jan.	Feb.	Mar.	Apr.	May	June
Conduct introductory meeting	X									
Collect and research information	X	X								
Identify additional resources		X	X							
Meet with Hardware Subcommittee				X		X				
Prepare specific recommendations per site							X			
Monitor physical preparations at each site							X		X	
Prepare evaluative report for District Committee										X

Enabling Objectives

Receive from the Curriculum Subcommittee the needs statement for teaching with microcomputers; i.e., needs requiring microcomputer laboratories, microcomputers for individual classrooms, microcomputers for dedicated applications.

Identify the schools that already house microcomputers and the location(s) of that hardware.

Determine the location and number of new and/or additional microcomputers in each school (K–12) relative to plans of the Curriculum Subcommittee.

Provide for corresponding software storage facilities in conjunction with the direction taken by the Software Subcommittee.

Establish the furniture and environmental needs, including those of peripherals, to support the microcomputer implementation.

Verify the feasibility of the microcomputer locations chosen for each school in terms of space, electrical outlets, anti-static carpeting, security, personnel, equipment mobility, and other considerations.

Estimate the costs per school to prepare the designated physical setting for the installation of the microcomputer(s).

Update planning, based on projected school closings and schools in transition during this planning phase.

During the year the subcommittees are at work, the district-level committee members continue to meet and monitor the progress of the work of each subcommittee. It may be that subcommittee reports will be brought to the district committee by members who have been serving as liaison, or the total subcommittee may be asked to appear before the district committee. The district is responsible for investigating resources and options available to the district, as well as for attending local and national conferences dealing with computers. Its findings can affect any of the subcommittees' work. Similarly, as the overall plan's progress is monitored, the committee may find that new issues have developed which it must address.

A "sample activity" which the district committee might address is the district-level policy regarding after-school-hours usage of microcomputers. Such a matter could affect some of the subcommittees' plans as well. The subcommittees' action plans should be evaluated annually and revised if necessary.

School Library Media Center as a Microcomputer Resource Center

When the school library media center encompasses the microcomputer resource center, it has been an integral part of a district's overall plan. The location has been so designated because library media specialists participated on the various subcommittees. Beginning with the traditional role, the school library media center can supply patrons with computer reference materials in any format and related resource information. As microcomputers are added, either at isolated stations in the library media center proper or as a group of microcomputers is installed in the center's adjacent classroom, centers will continue to be a place in which students can supplement their classroom learning, either by doing their computer homework or by locating additional information on disks (or doing special assignments).

Circulation in the library computer center will be in the form of computer hardware and software. Similarly, certain functions will have to be performed with the computer software, as is done with any print or nonprint materials—ordering, reviewing, purchasing, cataloging, processing, distribution, storage, maintenance, and possibly replacement. Computer equipment maintenance, instruction in its operation, and security will also be procedures the center personnel must develop carefully. Library media specialists must also research the literature and devise methods of performing these functions as related to microcomputers, their particular setting, and projected uses.

If the library media specialist goes beyond the traditional functions and uses the microcomputer for library management purposes (e.g., student overdues, automated cataloging), further investigation and planning will be needed. If access to online databases will be provided, the library media center must carefully lay the groundwork for this service as well. Such planning must be concurrent with the total district's plans. Special operations, relevant to certain school sites, should also be included.

The establishment of a district-wide microcomputer preview center in the first year of an implementation plan is suggested to aid each subcommittee in its work and to avoid duplication of cost and effort. If one room in a central location is available, with ample parking space, security, and adjacent school district staff to serve at least as gatekeepers, a preview center is feasible.

With minimal physical preparations, such as additional electric outlets, furniture, and storage units, a room could be converted into a preview center. All vendors could be directed to the center to display their equipment and schedule demonstrations. A variety of microcomputers from various manufacturers should be represented so that the subcommittees can arrive at equitable decisions. In addition, all software that is being considered for possible use in the district can be housed and previewed at the center. A file of written evaluations, completed by each person examining a software program, can also be maintained here, as well as files of published reviews, such as those of the Educational Products Information Exchange (EPIE).

The organization and operation of this center can provide insight for library media specialists into the possible problems which might arise, unique to microcomputer hardware and software management. Ample time will exist for solutions to be devised *before* microcomputer implementation within each library media center. Again, the establishment and operation of a district preview center must be planned by each district to meet its needs.

Selecting Software

E. Blanche Woolls

A survey of a national cross-section of 4,200 teachers and 1,000 principals, re-ported in the October 1983 issue of *Educational Computer Magazine,* found the attitudes of educators to be positive toward microcomputers in the classroom. More than 50 percent of the teachers who said that they had access to them indi-cated that they were users of microcomputers. This confirmed the need for teach-ers to have quality software available. Some reservations were indicated about the availability of hardware for student use and concern about the quality and quantity of available software. However, before software is selected, a decision must be made concerning the content to be taught. In addition, other questions which should be addressed include the following:

1. Is the microcomputer the most efficient way to present the information? One must consider that the pencil and paper workbook page provides drill and practice for all students at the same time. They will not be required to wait in line to complete the exercise on the limited number of microcom-puters which may be available in the classroom.
2. Would another method have been quicker, more efficient, more effective? Some microcomputer programs require an adult, seated beside the child, to assist in interpreting the program, in manipulating the peripherals, or in understanding the commands. It would be difficult to imagine a teacher and student in a one-to-one situation with a microcomputer interrupting that interaction. A film or a filmstrip may present the information more effectively for a larger group than can see the microcomputer terminal.

One must also remember that not all students learn in the same way. Many computer-assisted instruction programs are sequential in presentation. These pro-grams may interest some students only for a short period of time, and they may quickly become bored with this method of presentation. Other students, who enjoy learning how things operate, may be more interested in how the machine runs than what is running on it. These students would rather take the microcomputer apart than work the problems on the terminal.

When the microcomputer is the most efficient means for presenting the topic, one must be concerned about the availability of hardware and software, and concerns about the quality and quantity of software are real but need not be permanent. Selecting quality microcomputer software is not as difficult as it was when the microcomputer first arrived in the school. Not only is the quantity of software growing, but producers are becoming more familiar with the needs of educators. More and more good-quality software is becoming available. Unfortunately, this does not mean that software of questionable value and/or poor quality will no longer exist. This is not unique to microcomputer software. Bad books continue to be published and poor films are still produced.

Before purchase, all courseware should be evaluated by predetermined selection criteria. The basic criteria for selection of microcomputer software have been suggested by many individuals, such as school district personnel, project staff who have received government funding to establish software review centers, and members of professional associations who have drawn up guidelines. Checklists have been developed and revised to offer selection criteria for general use or for specific areas of the curriculum. Access to reviews in periodicals for teachers and school library media specialists (*Booklist* and *The Book Report* are two which carry regular reviews), as well as lists of recommended software and guidebooks to quality software, are available to help school library media specialists make wise selections of titles to purchase.

With all the information available, one might debate the need for more words on this topic. However, the selection of software should be the first consideration in developing a program for the use of microcomputers in schools, and the selection of appropriate learning materials has always been the responsibility of the school library media specialist. This specialist, as manager of the other curriculum materials in the school library media center, is in control of the media budgets for his or her school. They will control the final purchase decisions for this new type of media. Coordinating purchase through a single person will be essential as costs for software rise.

Forecasters predict that the cost of software will become the major investment for any microcomputer program. At this time, microcomputers with enough memory to accomplish a wide variety of functions are still expensive enough that few schools have very many microcomputers. This cost is constantly decreasing as new technology lowers the cost of manufacture while increasing the capability of the machines. Purchasing the wide variety of software for various needs will be the escalating budget item.

The newness of this technology and its enthusiastic acceptance by students, teachers, and school library media specialists have created a market for good software. With this newly developed media format, it has become necessary to learn additional selection techniques. It is the responsibility of the school library media specialist to learn how to choose software which will avoid the dangers of "soulless drudgery and mindless entertainment."

It is the further responsibility of the library media specialist to assist the teacher in the careful selection of the best learning tool for the student in each curricular area. If that tool is the microcomputer, the most appropriate software will spell the difference between success and failure, not only for the student but also for perception of the quality of this technology application. It is time to select the microcomputer when it is proved to be the best tool to get the job done.

The first difficulty in selecting software is to determine if a package will run on the school's equipment. It may not surprise many readers to learn that microcomputer hardware is no more compatible than most other types of audiovisual equipment. What will work on one brand of microcomputer may not work on a competitor's. Once it is determined that a package will "run," other criteria must be considered.

When the right brand of equipment is available, one must analyze the system to see if enough equipment has been provided. (This may mean the *size of memory*—how much storage capacity is available for one particular microcomputer—needed to run the program, or the type of *peripherals* needed.) Just as one must have a cassette recorder and a filmstrip projector to use a multimedia kit, certain required peripherals dictate the choice of microcomputer programs. Many programs such as teacher management programs, which need to have student scores for easy viewing, require a *printer*. (All word processing programs require printers.) Programs which require sound may not work without *speech or sound synthesizers*. Other programs require a *joystick* to move the figures around the screen. Thus, availability of peripherals affects the selection of software.

One difficulty in selecting software is to locate what is available on the market. A great deal of software is being produced, but information about what is available, where to locate it, how much it costs, or how to see the programs is not widely known. The expansion of exhibitors at professional association meetings, "fairs," and the sharing of successful projects and programs is alleviating this problem. However, the ability to preview still presents a problem.

Preview

One of the major problems is securing microcomputer materials for preview. After school library media specialists see ads, or favorable reviews, or read brochures about a program, they often find that companies are unwilling to provide a preview of their products. Much of this reluctance is due to the ease of copying and reproducing programs.

Many software manufacturers *do* provide preview copies, but certainly they are in the minority. Others offer "sample" programs which do not really substitute for examining the entire programs. Few school library media specialists are willing to order a book based solely upon reading three paragraphs provided by the publisher. For the same reason, partial microcomputer programs do not allow analysis of the potential for use in the classroom. Many school district personnel will not purchase software *unless* they can preview, and strong consideration should be given to such a policy, even though reviewing sources are increasing steadily in number and quality of their reviews.

Software programs are available in two categories—protected and unprotected. If a program is unprotected, it may be duplicated very easily. Duplication of unprotected but copyrighted programs should be restricted to making a backup copy at the local school level, in case the original is inadvertently destroyed (in either storage or use). Making a backup copy does *not* include copying for other schools in a district—although some software manufacturers allow such duplication for an entire district and state this in their product promotions. Others do not, and duplication then becomes a violation of the copyright law. The seeming lack of concern for this violation of copyright is one reason why many software manufacturers are not interested in producing microcomputer software for schools. The business community is more likely to purchase one copy of each program for each microcomputer it owns, while educators seem to swap software readily. Businesses are also less likely to modify a selected program.

Copyright

Producers of microcomputer software must be rewarded for their investment by selling as many copies as possible. However, microcomputer software is often very easy to copy. Almost as soon as a producer has built an "ironclad" program, a clever computer user develops a means to break the protective features. This conduct is perceived by many producers to be the rule, rather than the exception, with educators. School library media specialists have been jealous guardians of copyright. It is hoped that they can continue to discourage the illegal reproduction of microcomputer software and its accompanying documentation. One regional service center has entered into a contract with a manufacturer for the rights to duplicate microcomputer software and the accompanying documentation for schools in that service area, and the other regional media directors are sponsoring support for legislation to obtain the rights for the entire state. The literature should report such methods in the future.

Revising Software

Some teachers wish to modify programs to suit the special needs of their students. If a program is protected, this will not be possible. If it is unprotected, the teacher or school library media specialist must have some knowledge of programming, in the language of the package, if changes are to be made. Many manufacturers do not wish to have their packages modified. These packages have been developed with planned sequences, and modification may destroy the intent of the producer. This characteristic is not unique to this type of audiovisual material; it is also true of 16mm films and videotapes. Attempting to modify a 16mm film will destroy the producer's planned sequence and will scramble the sound track. The next teacher who attempts to use a modified program may believe that the package is poorly produced, rather than locally revised.

Replacing Software

A final "housekeeping" decision has to do with the need for replacement of damaged programs. Programs should be purchased for which there is some type of warranty; that is, the school library media specialist should be able to make a backup copy of any disk or cassette. Unfortunately, most educational software publishers do not want copies made of their software, a policy intended to prevent unauthorized copying. However, copyright laws allow purchasers to print one backup copy of the tape or diskette, and this should be allowed by the publisher and honored by the purchaser. It is very important, because tapes and diskettes are easily damaged. If they will not permit making one backup copy, publishers should offer the backup copy at a low cost—and not charge the same as for the purchase of the original. If possible, tapes and disks should be selected from companies that offer at least a 90-day warranty.

Expanding Teacher Awareness through Cooperative Selection

Two human problems must be overcome if microcomputers are to become a part of the curriculum. The first is to overcome the reluctance of teachers to participate in selection of materials for the school library media center, and the second is to get classroom teachers interested in this new technology. Participating in choosing software will expand teachers' knowledge about the potential of microcomputer use by students, as well as for their own management functions, and may help them become enthusiastic users. Other teachers, though willing to use the equipment, may not understand its capabilities, and they may expect more than the microcomputer is designed to give. Helping preview software may give them an understanding of the limitations of memory and the need for peripherals for some software packages. It should also help them decide if it is better to purchase commercial programs or attempt to write their own.

   Teachers will become better evaluators if they and the school library media specialist define the selection criteria for all microcomputer software. Applying these criteria to several programs will increase knowledge about each critical area. Next, a *very brief* evaluation form should be developed, or an existing form adapted, for use by teachers. All teachers should then be given inservice training to acquaint them with the criteria for selection and the differences between choosing microcomputer software and other types of media.

Selection Criteria

General criteria which are applied to all information which is to be placed in any school library media center and is applicable to the selection of microcomputer software include accuracy of content. Microcomputer software must be not only free of content errors, but must not have misspellings. Misspellings often creep into the instructions on the microcomputer screen, if not in the program text.

The criterion ''authenticity'' may not seem, at first, to be as appropriate or difficult for the microcomputer since many consider this format only as a screen with letters and numbers, rather than the pictures and sound they must consider when reviewing a filmstrip. However, the microcomputer has both sound and graphics capability which must be used efficiently as well as correctly. A program which asks students to identify block letters and numbers, or the states of the United States, should picture those letters, numbers, or states clearly.

Relevance in choice of program must be equally matched to relevance in use of programs. Purchasing a program which is highly recommended by evaluators and popular with students and teachers is a first step. An example of such a program is Oregon Trail, available from numerous publishers and public domain sources. This program, which simulates a pioneer journey across the United States to Oregon, presents hardships encountered by a pioneer, and students must make difficult decisions concerning food, ammunition, and trade. The program can contribute to a study of the westward movement, if used properly in context and the teacher includes other learning activities in the unit. Because of its ''gaming'' element, Oregon Trail may easily become the equivalent of the ''Friday afternoon film''—not the educational simulation intended by its designers.

Schoolteachers and media specialists must always be concerned with the ''difficulty level'' of materials. No student wishes to have the instructions read aloud because the vocabulary is on an eleventh grade level and the program plays concepts which are taught in the sixth grade. Conversely, simple programs will not attract the ''slow'' student in the eleventh grade. The microcomputer will not appeal any more than an ''easy'' book.

Microcomputer programs, like multimedia kits and other forms of media, should have adequate documentation. This does not mean that the student should be required to read the documentation to make the program run, but that the school library media specialist and the teacher should be provided with course objectives, a description of the content of the program, directions for modifying the program, and any changes which can be made. Good microcomputer programs have excellent documentation.

The media specialist must also decide if the presentation of information is not available elsewhere in the collection. Many microcomputer programs are merely workbooks with practice problems and, as such, would seldom be considered for purchase. On the other hand, their unique qualities may make it appropriate to add a microcomputer program even though the media center already houses information on the topic. It may be that the additional program should be relegated to a second-priority purchase and other areas be selected before this program.

While the above are common criteria for choosing information, the next are unique to the microcomputer or present different aspects because of its capabilities. A microcomputer program may flash instructions too rapidly to be read by the intended audience. Although the vocabulary is at the proper level, the timing is not. Most programs should treat the different capabilities of learners in appropriate ways. The capability of the microcomputer to *branch* is one of its superb characteristics. Programs should reflect this capability and be able to reach a variety of learners with a speed and difficulty level which is matched to their first responses.

Children can become mesmerized by television, almost to the point of becoming hermits. Likewise, they can be totally immersed in microcomputer programs, so that they become isolated from other children. It is wise to look for programs which allow students to interact with other students. Discussion with students before choices are made will increase learning, and such programs are to be given priority.

Many microcomputer programs have not been thoroughly *debugged*—the process which makes sure a program runs correctly in all of its sequences. Strange as it may seem, one program loop or subroutine may not have been thoroughly tested by the manufacturer. In these cases, the producer should be notified and an exchange made to correct the error.

A major criterion for use of a microcomputer is that it be "user friendly." This means that the student should be able to use the program with little or no assistance from an aide, the teacher, or the library media specialist. If assistance is required because the vocabulary is too difficult, a substitute program should be chosen. If the program has few instructions or those that are provided do not lead the student easily through the program, it is not "user friendly" and an alternative should be selected.

Most quality programs offer students a *prompt* or a *help screen* at every point during a program. (If a prompt is given, does the help screen really assist the user in continuing the program?) Unless truly helpful hints are available, a program will not be useful to many students.

Good microcomputer programs are capable of being modified, if the content is such that changes are logical (e.g., different spellings of words, level of difficulty of math problems). Programs also often scramble the sequence of questions so that students cannot memorize a set of response letters or numbers.

Microcomputer programs are unique in that they can branch. The student who responds with numerous correct answers may be moved into more difficult questions by the microcomputer, while the student with incorrect answers may have to review and respond again.

The selector must also use care to decide if sound would be distracting to other students. When sound is either a reward or an indication of failure, an entire class may become aware of a student's success or failure. Such an awareness is not usually in the best interest of learning.

The reviewer should take into consideration the *menu*, or listing, of a program's or lesson's parts. It may appear on the screen as a topic outline. Better-quality programs begin with a master menu that allows users to select the section with which to begin their work. The program should contain *submenus* throughout, but the last question on the submenu should be a request to halt the program or to return to the main menu.

Information should be given promptly. The speed of the arcade game has created a level of expectation for children. If the microcomputer is slow to react, and no indication of this is given on the screen, students will become bored with the time lapse.

Microcomputer program selectors must always keep in mind that these programs should take advantage of the computer's unique capabilities. Violating these qualities will make the microcomputer an object of ''soulless drudgery.'' In the nonmicrocomputer world, pages and pages of workbooks and texts are often transferred into miles and miles of purple ditto sheets. Initial experience with them, in the earliest grades, has long since ceased to interest many children. A mere workbook, with screen after screen of problems to solve, with no variation in difficulty, will not enhance drill and practice beyond the first stages of microcomputer usage. In fact, many students would prefer to do workbook-style drill and practice at their desks, rather than search the keyboard to enter answers.

A microcomputer will

1. Interest students enough to continue drill and practice, if reinforcement is entertaining.
2. Keep the students' attention somewhat longer than many other learning devices, including the average lecturing human.
3. Provide personalized reinforcement. (Use of a student's name is the primary mechanism, while flashing stars, ringing bells, and smiling faces also provide rewards.)
4. Branch to allow the student with correct answers to move into more difficult questions, or allow the student with incorrect answers to review and respond again.
5. Arouse and instantly reinforce competitive spirits by displaying who in a group of students was fastest with the most correct answers during a segment of the program.

6. Keep a record of scores for the teacher, who can then easily determine how to reinforce or review and when to move to another unit.
7. Make instant calculations (when a concept is more important than the mathematical manipulations; e.g., economic concepts are more important in the program Lemonade Stand than keeping an accounting record.)
8. Allow rapid information retrieval. (Locating citations and securing abstracts is instantaneous, in comparison to manual searches.)

Some otherwise excellent microcomputer programs have what might be called "mechanical flaws," which greatly detract from the programs' value as a learning resource or teaching tool. For instance, some microcomputer programs

1. May not allow the student to exit the programs easily. For some programs there is no "shutting the book" and thereby ending the program—only turning off the machine.
2. May not load rapidly enough to keep the attention of the student. Long pauses with a blank screen can distract students and disrupt the flow of learning.
3. May not be the best use of the format. Dull drill and practice, in any format, is still dull.
4. May not be designed for the "amateur" typist. With some programs, an error on the keyboard may *abort* the program. Since many high school users, as well as most elementary school children, may not be expert typists, such an event can be frustrating. Time is lost in restarting the program, and may increase one's fear for attempting the program another time.

This medium, as do other audiovisual formats, may encourage misuse. Microcomputer programs are not a substitute for planned instruction, but must be carefully integrated into curriculum units. They are not a replacement for supervised instructional time. Student use of the microcomputer requires close supervision, or students may become confused, bored, or begin to play games after completing an exercise.

Sharing Software Selection Information

Because of the dramatic increase in the availability of good-quality software and selection aids, the school library media specialist is now able to work from the needs of the curriculum to purchase the most suitable software, rather than forced to purchase any acceptable software package simply because it is all that is available. Also, the attention given to the microcomputer may force school library media specialists to use it because that is what is expected.

This may take the media specialist back to the periodical literature, to well-planned sessions at professional meetings, and to inservice workshops in districts and regions. When microcomputer software is used in creative ways to support units in the curriculum—perhaps with other types of media, as well as the textbook or trade book—this information must be disseminated to a wide audience.

Disseminating information about successes places another burden on busy, creative, and successful school library media specialists to make sure that they share their knowledge about effective programs with others. Reading about program uses would point out specific packages which might apply to more than one area. This will speed up the time when selection of software will become totally dependent upon a *specific* curricular use. Software will then no longer be purchased first and squeezed into or attached to a unit later, often with marginal application.

Sharing Software Purchases

While most library media specialists control the media budgets for their schools, the microcomputer is not considered as media in all schools' software purchasing budgets. Selecting microcomputer software includes anticipating the awarding of funds for software to departments by administrators. School library media specialists must be ready with examples of the best in all curriculum areas so that teachers do not resort to publishers' catalogs or ads in teachers' journals to spend their allocations. Being helpful may speed the transfer of microcomputer software purchasing into the media center, where it belongs.

One way this may evolve may be through the purchase of copyright clearance. Some regional centers (and entire states) are acquiring the rights to quality computer programs and related support materials. In many instances this means the purchase of copyright clearance for duplication of microcomputer programs for school districts. They are also seeking programs which are in the public domain.

Since the emphasis on selection has advanced from selection of programs merely to allow the microcomputer to be used for something beyond programming and has advanced to specific curricular uses, it is now time to consider the need for "weeding" programs. Some removal of programs which are no longer useful may be done through the misuse of disks or cassettes. If no backup copy was maintained, one can begin the application of selection criteria immediately to decide whether or not to replace a destroyed item. The industry is so new that very little software has "gone out of print." One need only confirm that a program meets the selection criteria and fills a curricular need before reordering.

When a software package is not used in an area of the curriculum, choices must be made annually about retaining such software. The ease of storing this format may add to the reluctance of many to remove a package for any reason. Microcomputer programs will become dated, lose their relevancy, or be replaced by newer, better versions; and this area of the media must be assessed as often and rigorously as other formats.

In the replacement-weeding process, one would hope that all school library media specialists are moving into diskettes. Cassettes, while requiring much less expensive hardware, are too slow. The valuable teaching/learning time lost waiting for a cassette to load is no longer acceptable. More and more programs are being developed for disk. It will only be the need for voice or sound that will keep cassettes "attached" to microcomputers.

In making plans to switch from cassettes to disk drives, the school library media specialist must begin making plans for upgrading whatever systems are now in the media center. Rapid technological changes will not allow any educator to feel complacent about any microcomputer program currently in place. Future software will demand larger memory and expanded capability of the hardware. Also, new brands of microcomputers will appear and offer different programs which will probably not be compatible. Expansion plans must be made now.

Selecting new titles for use by teachers and students has long been one of the more pleasant tasks for the school library media specialist. The need to choose the best use of the available microcomputer software is a challenge all school library media specialists should welcome.

Selecting a Microcomputer

Roger R. Flynn

This chapter presumes that the library media specialist has read articles describing the brand names on the market and that the reader has some beginning knowledge of the types of microcomputers available. Articles with this information are available in all computer magazines and many library publications.

Selectors of microcomputer systems may not always be the persons who actually operate the systems, the "end users." School library media specialists may only choose, rather than use—or train to use—the system. However, it is important that the library media specialist, as buyer, understand and apply the *systems* approach, rather than select the least expensive equipment.

The factors to be considered in selecting a microcomputer system divide along the traditional categories: hardware and software. The more important of the two is software, which is necessary for any system to function. Hardware is the *pre-condition* to achieving this functionality. Despite this fact, it seems that the hardware is the major obstacle in selection of a machine because of its more remote concepts and vocabulary. The software, more akin to goals and needs, is understandable. Hence, this analysis begins with discussion of the machinery rather than the utility of the system.

The major components of a microcomputer system are the *central processing unit* (CPU), the *main memory,* the *input and output devices, secondary storage,* and the *data transfer paths and data communication devices.* Each of these will be discussed in turn.

The CPU

Two of the primary concerns in selection of a processing unit are the processing speed and the flexibility and power of the instruction set. The first of these, pro-

25

cessing speed, is usually expressed in terms of *instructions per second,* for example, 1 million instructions per second (MIPS). The number of instructions that can be executed in 1 second depends on the clock speed of the computer. All events in the life of the computer, such as fetching instructions and data, then executing instructions, occur at the speed of the clock. Hence, a computer with a "faster clock" is potentially a faster processor of instructions. The term *potentially* is added because it normally takes more than a single clock cycle to execute a given instruction.

If the computer uses more cycles to execute an instruction, then the machine that has a higher clock rate may actually have a lower effective rate of processing. One example in which the number of cycles per instruction can vary is the use of an *8-bit* bus versus a *16-bit* bus to access data. (A *bus* is a set of lines on which bit values can be transferred; the term *bus* is used because the lines transport the bits as passengers.) An 8-bit microcomputer would require an 8-bit line to transfer one byte of data. Here is a diagram of an 8-bit line.

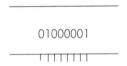

01000001

Most microcomputers that are manufactured today have 16-bit *words,* locations where data is stored. However, some have an 8-bit bus, while others have a 16-bit bus. To process data 16 bits wide with an 8-bit bus takes two trips, that is, two clock cycles. To access 16-bit data with a 16-bit bus takes one clock cycle. Hence, the machine with the 16-bit bus gets the job done twice as fast as the machine with the 8-bit bus.

The point of the buses is that the clock time, which is advertised by the manufacturers, is not a perfect guide to the effective speed of a machine. Knowing the instructions executed per second is a somewhat more reliable guide, although even this measure has flaws. Some instructions, such as "multiply" (rather than "add"), take longer to perform. Commands that access peripheral devices, such as a disk or data from the keyboard, called "reads" and "writes," usually take a hundred or several hundred milliseconds on a microcomputer system, or about 50 to 100 thousands times as long to execute as an "internal" interaction. Hence, one needs to know a sampling of the instructions of the microcomputer, as well as a sampling of the types of instructions one's programs will use.

The flexibility and power of the instruction set examines such questions as "How easy is it to do a multiply or divide?" or "floating point arithmetic?" Some processors have hardware that multiplies directly; others use a process termed *repeated addition*. In repeated additions (5*3 is 3 "adds" of 5), execution takes longer than a single hardware execution. Similarly, if one's machine has floating point hardware (to handle numbers such as 4.3, or *real* numbers), it can execute floating point instructions faster than a machine that uses a combination of integer arithmetic and a program to simulate the floating point arithmetic.

Another question in considering the central processor is the size and number of its arithmetic registers (*accumulators*). The size of an arithmetic register determines the size of numbers that can be added, multiplied, or otherwise manipulated by the processing unit. An 8-bit accumulator can hold numbers as large as 255 (2 raised to the eighth power minus 1). This is not a large number for any application. In order to handle larger numbers, microcomputers with 8-bit registers must rely on software programs to manipulate more than a single word in order to do the arithmetic or even to represent the number. A 16-bit register can hold numbers as large as 65,535, so that special manipulations are not necessary for many applications. Current microcomputer technology tends toward 16-bit registers, both for the arithmetic registers and for the memory registers or storage locations. Some manufacturers are moving toward 32-bit words, at which point one is approaching the power of minicomputers in ease of representation and manipulating numbers.

The number of arithmetic registers also affects the speed and convenience with which computations can be executed. On most machines, data must be moved from the main memory to the accumulator or arithmetic register before work can be done. If a machine has a single accumulator, a good deal of time is spent moving data back and forth between the work area (the accumulator) and the storage area (main memory). If there are several arithmetic registers, jobs are executed faster.

In summary, speed in a microcomputer is affected by the number of accumulators and the size of bus (8 bit, 16 bit, or 32 bit). The overall effect of these capabilities is response time, i.e., the length of time the user must wait for a command to be carried out. In a practical sense, speed may or may not be critical, and for many instructional programs, response time is not a major factor. If a math problem has just been answered by a student, waiting 10 milliseconds, instead of 5, will probably not be noticed. Text applications, such as *word processors,* are not usually affected greatly by CPU speed, but are affected by access time to and from the disk drive.

Programs where CPU speed makes a great deal of difference usually involve numerical manipulations. Library management programs are good examples where CPU speed becomes important. Circulation systems, automated catalogs, and spreadsheets should be selected carefully and their hardware requirements screened. In these cases, true 16- and 32-bit processors are clearly superior, all else being equal.

Main Memory

The primary question in regard to main memory is its size and its expandability. The size of the main memory determines the size of the program that can be handled. When main memory is limited, portions of a large program may be brought in a piece at a time, but this complicates the programming effort and can lead to a less efficient performance. One technique is to divide a program into self-contained modules which are relatively independent of other modules. In this way, communication between disk and main memory is minimized.

The size of the main memory is governed by the size of the *address bus*, the lines or bit paths on which the CPU places the "address" of the memory location to be accessed. If the bus has 8 lines, there may be only 256 memory locations (2** 8 = 256); the locations will be numbered 0 through 255). Clearly, there will not be enough space to do anything worthwhile. A larger address space may be achieved with an 8-bit address by allowing addresses to be formed in two parts or two clock cycles, with the first 8 bits forming the selection of one out of 256 *segments*, the second 8 bits selecting a single word (or byte) out of the selected segment. Thus:

Segment 0-255	Word 0-255

Creating the address in this fashion expands the address space to 256*256, or 65,536 locations, but it does so at the expense of processing time.

A 16-bit bus provides access to 65,536 locations (64K) in 1 clock cycle, but even this is not a very large address space. Hence, even systems with a 16-bit bus will often provide a memory management module that uses a few extra bits to select among several 64K segments. The "extra" bits will increase the number of bits necessary to specify an address, increasing the number of bytes necessary to create an instruction.

A good rule to follow for choosing a microcomputer is to buy as large a main memory as can be afforded. When a smaller memory, such as 64K or 128K, is chosen, try to buy a microcomputer which allows the addition of memory modules (or *boards*) in increments of some fixed size, perhaps 64K or 128K each, and adding boards as needed. One then needs to ask questions about the minimum amount of money needed to configure the system and the cost of *upgrades,* or additional boards.

The size of memory is particularly critical in considering "packages" that one wishes to use. It may be that a particular package needs 64K in order to run. In this case, anyone who wishes to use such a software program will need to purchase a system with at least that capacity.

One distinction that is often made in discussing microcomputers is the difference between *random access memory* (RAM) and *read only memory* (ROM). As Wakerly indicates, RAM is often referred to as *read/write memory* (RWM) since the microcomputer can both read from it and write into it;[1] however, RAM is a holdover from its name, before ROM became prevalent. Read only memory is used to store programs such as the operating system or the BASIC interpreter. When the system is turned on, a mechanism to read the ROM is activated. This "boots" or "brings up" the system.

ROM is not useful for creating programs since one cannot write to the ROM. It is simply a permanent copy of the system software (permanent data files). Hence, if one says the system has 128K of memory, 64K of ROM, and 64K of RAM, one knows that it has only 64K of usable memory, where *usable* is interpreted as the memory that can be used to load and run packages or to develop programs. It is always necessary to know the memory size in terms of RAM, not ROM.

Another useful question is how much usable RAM a microcomputer has. Manufacturers often will take a large piece of the advertised RAM space for various machine functions, so that, in a 64K machine, only 48K of usable RAM might be available for a software program.

Two other terms define ROM's relatives, PROM and EPROM. PROM stands for *programmable read only memory.* It means memory that is read only, but allows the bits to be "set" by the user. It usually consists of electrical elements that are initially all connected, often by a wire with a fuse on it, indicating the 1 (or zero) state. The programmer programs the memory by "blowing the fuses," thus creating zeros. After the memory is programmed in this fashion, it is "left alone" forever. That is ROM.

EPROM is *erasable programmable read only memory.* It uses a different technology, creating ones or zeros by isolating electrons in a particular area. These electrons can be "freed," erasing the 1s, by exposing the storage medium to an energy source that "excites" the electrons, such as ultraviolet light.

Some microcomputers come outfitted with programs permanently stored in ROM. Usually BASIC is stored there, but some microcomputers have word processors, database managers, and spreadsheets stored permanently. When the microcomputer is turned on, these programs are available instantly and need not be loaded from disk. A number of the small, portable microcomputers have ROM programs in addition to the RAM.

The trend in today's market is to build microcomputers with larger and larger main memories. In just a few years, the average microcomputer memory has increased from 48K to 128K. This trend seems likely to continue and is a positive development for library media applications. Larger memories mean that larger

---

[1]John F. Wakerly, *Microcomputer Architecture and Programming* (New York: John Wiley & Sons, 1981).

files can be manipulated, such as on-order files, large indexes, or large word-processed documents. A simple example may suffice. The popular program, Apple Writer, can process documents containing approximately 10,000 characters in a 64K Apple. If the Apple memory is expanded to 128K, the same program can handle documents of 28,000 characters in length.

In summary, two rules for purchase of a microcomputer are essential with reference to main memory. First, a microcomputer must have a large enough memory to handle the desired software program. Second, it is wise to buy as much memory as possible, or at least be sure that main memory can be expanded easily to increase the capabilities of the present software to fit a future application.

Peripherals

Peripheral devices can be divided into two types: those used for input/output and those used for storage. We treat the input/output devices first.

The most common input device is the *keyboard.* It may be attached to a cathode ray tube (CRT) or *monitor* or *video display unit* (VDU) or a television screen; alternatively, it may be attached to a *hard-copy terminal,* a device that produces output on paper. It is ubiquitous.

The question one wishes to ask about the keyboard is its ease of use and the extensiveness of the character set it allows one to use. Ease of use is determined by several characteristics: its physical detachability; the placement of frequently used keys, such as the shift key and the return or *enter* key; the size of the keys; the use of the *function* keys and their interpretation; and, finally, whether keys are used at all.

In regard to detachability, the general rule is that a detachable keyboard is preferable to one that is not detachable. It allows one to change one's sitting position easily, hence avoiding fatigue. The placement of critical keys, such as the return, is a little more problematic. One needs to use a few different keyboards to develop a preference. However, the typing of a few commands will generally reveal gross inconveniences in the design. In any case, one does not usually have a wide choice in regard to the keyboard. The manufacturers of various computers will usually offer only one or a few keyboard options, so that one is fairly "locked in" once one has chosen a particular vendor to supply the processing unit. It is, however, useful to be aware of the general issue.

The size of the keys is a factor in ease of typing. If they are too small or spaced too closely together, it can be difficult to hit the right key and to avoid hitting two keys at once. Of course, one can go to the other extreme as well. It is said that one manufacturer, reacting to criticism that the return key was too small, designed a keyboard with a return key that could be "ridden over by a Mack truck."

Function keys are useful for entering frequently used commands. For example, one might have function keys for the commands LIST or RUN in BASIC. Instead of typing the three or four letters for these commands, one would hit a single key that has been designated the "run" key or the "list" key. If function keys are provided, it is usually preferable that they are *programmable*. That is, users can set the meaning according to their specific needs.

Similar to function keys is the use of a *numeric keypad*. A numeric keypad has only ten digits, 0 through 9, and can be manipulated by one hand. If one enters an extensive amount of numeric data, this can speed processing. If not, it is irrelevant, although the cost for a numeric keypad will be built into the price of the terminal, whether the keypad will be used or not. All bells and whistles cost money.

General-purpose keyboards are preferable to special-purpose keyboards, except in specific applications. Special-purpose keyboards can speed processing in specific applications, such as cataloging books or making hotel reservations. However, they cannot be used to communicate with systems other than those for which they were designed. This is usually not an issue in purchasing off-the-shelf microcomputers since these usually use a general-purpose keyboard. Microcomputers that have been customized for a particular application, such as an OCLC terminal, might have a customized keyboard—but that is a separate question which is of interest only to people who work in that application area. Customized designs will generally be more expensive since they have a smaller potential market. They are less flexible by definition; both the cost and the loss of flexibility pay dividends in efficiency of operations in application.

Some microcomputer manufacturers save costs in the development of their keyboard by eliminating the physically moving keys in favor of pressure-sensitive *touch keys*. These are generally not as convenient to use as the more standard keyboards, although they are quite satisfactory in some areas, such as computer-aided design (CAD) and computer-aided manufacture (CAM) systems, which are instances of customized systems.

The size and flexibility of the *character set* is another important question to the purchaser of a terminal. This question interacts with the capability of the output portion of the system: "Can the display unit display Greek letters? Subscripts? Superscripts? Special graphics characters?" It will also interact with the capabilities of the software: "Can the text forematter handle various fonts? Various line levels for printing (to handle subscripts and superscripts)?"

The general idea, however, is similar to that used in choosing typewriters: Is an equal sign needed? A Greek sigma? And does the terminal allow one?

Mice and Other Creatures

An input device that is gaining great popularity is the *mouse*. The mouse is a box-like device that is manipulated by one's hand. It is mounted on rollers that are able to detect vertical and horizontal motion, and one uses the mouse to move the *cur-*

sor on the microcomputer screen. It is usually used in conjunction with a *menu-driven* system, the "menus" consisting of icons rather than a list of alphanumeric entries. The icons represent capabilities of the system, such as painting pictures, editing, and others. One moves the cursor to the icon that represents the function one desires, then presses a button that "activates" the mouse. This causes the microcomputer to read the position of the cursor and determine what the user desires.

Another feature of import in using the mouse is *trigger keys.* Some systems offer mice with a single key, others with two or three. The mice with a few keys, rather than one, are easier to manipulate when more than one action is necessary in entering a command, although one needs to remember which key does what. If the library media specialist has the choice of using a mouse only, keyboard controls only, or both simultaneously, the latter is superior and provides maximum flexibility.

Other Animals

Besides alphanumeric keyboards and mice, other input devices are *light pens, wands or bar-code readers, joysticks, imagers,* and the like. The light pen is equivalent to the mouse. It senses light from a video display unit and manipulates a cursor, or other objects, on the screen. Only the methods of manipulating differ. One points the pen to choose from menus, move objects, and so on. It is equivalent to the mouse in ease of use, especially in graphics-based systems, although the mouse is currently in the ascendency in the marketplace.

A joystick is not equivalent to either the mouse or the light pen. It is useful for interacting with games, where the analog motion of the stick parallels the analog motion required in the game. However, it is not accurate enough, in its granularity of motion, to be convenient in selecting objects on a screen.

Bar-code readers are special-purpose input devices which sense magnetic codes that are usually printed on a label. They are useful for reading product codes (such as those on grocery items) or book labels in the school library media center. They are not suitable for general-purpose input. Among the various bar-code readers, library media specialists should choose on the basis of reliability. Talk with owners of bar-code readers. Ask salespersons for names of customers, and ask others in the information community or other library media specialists.

Output Devices

The first distinction among output devices is whether they are hard copy or not. "Hard copy" is a euphemism for "paper output." In regard to microcomputers, the two most common output units are the video display unit and the printer.

Video Display Units. In considering video display units, one wants to know whether graphics capability is or is not available. Since much of the software developed for microcomputers is developed with graphics in mind, this is almost a must. The questions in regard to the display unit then become those of resolution and color, and, in conjunction with these questions, of the software available to take advantage of these features.

In regard to resolution, "more is better" is a key concept, although "more" is usually more expensive. The term *resolution* refers to the number of picture elements, dots or *pixels,* that can be lit on the screen in the horizontal and vertical directions. A resolution of 320 by 160 would have 320 dots in the horizontal direction, 160 vertical; resolution of 1024*1024 has over a million pixels, arranged in a square matrix.

Just as in print technology, such as newspaper photographs, the quality of pictures rises with the resolution factor. So do processing requirements. The screen must be drawn and "refreshed" from a *bit map* that represents what pixels should be on, which off, when the screen is "drawn." The memory required to hold the bit map and the input/output processing requirements of the CPU increase with the number of bits handled.

It is not the case that 1 bit in the bit map always represents a single pixel on the screen. This is true only if the screen pixels are monochrome (single color) and have only two intensities (on, off). If there is more than one color or more than two intensities, more than one bit will be devoted to each pixel. For example, if there are 3 colors (red, green, blue) and each is "on-off," one needs 3 bits per pixel. The color red would be represented as

$$R \quad G \quad B$$
$$1 \quad 0 \quad 0$$

Mixtures such as purple would have more than a single color lit:

$$R \quad G \quad B$$
$$1 \quad 0 \quad 1$$

The "palette" of on-off for R,G,B allows for only 8 distinct colors, ranging from black (0,0,0) to white (1,1,1). To achieve a more extensive palette, extra bits must be devoted to each pixel, specifying intensities of red, intensities of green, intensities of blue.

As the discussion indicates, one wishes to know whether the monitor is capable of color display or monochrome only. One can always have monochrome if one has color, but not vice versa. Color monitors are more expensive but allow for more pleasing variety to displays. Some users prefer monochrome displays for heavy usage because they usually have a sharper image. Vendors of microcomputers usually offer a limited range of monitors with their processors. Many processors are offered "unbundled," so that one can purchase the monitor separately. The question is best studied by examining monitor displays in person, similar to selection of a television set.

One question that is receiving a good deal of attention is the occurrence of fatigue, eyestrain, and the like in using video display units. The color of the screen, glare, flicker in the characters, the sitting position required by the monitor, and keyboard positioning can all contribute to ease of use or fatigue and discomfort. Research in human factors is attacking several of these problems, but the results do not seem definitive. (In fact, the experience of one of the author's secretaries has been directly contrary to "recommended" courses of action.) In any case, flexibility of color choice, good resolution, and movability (tilt, twist) of displays and keyboards allow one to vary the characteristics of the interaction enough to delay fatigue and reduce adaptation.

Printers. The questions in regard to *printers* are the quality of the output, the speed of the output, and the durability of the machine. The quality of output refers to the extensiveness of the character set as well as to the physical clarity of the characters printed. It also refers to the capability to have graphics as well as alphanumeric output. Sometimes the various features are antithetical to one another. For example, a *letter-quality* printer, as found in typewriters, provides clearer images than a *dot-matrix* printer. The dot matrix is a rectangular set of pins that are pushed out to form characters. Since the pins may be pushed out in any configuration, a dot matrix can print graphic images from the screen.

While laser printers are not readily available for the microcomputer, this technology should be understood by the library media specialist. Laser printers use various technologies, one of the most popular being a process similar to that used in photocopiers. The laser beam heats the paper where the alphanumeric characters, symbols, or graphics are to be drawn, and a carbon material is sprayed at the surface, adhering to the heated portions of the paper. These printers are more expensive than the dot-matrix or letter-quality printers available at this time.

The cost of printers ranges from $200 to the price of a home. Those appropriate to microcomputers range from $200 to $2,000 or $3,000. The technology is rapidly changing. Laser printers that were available only for $20,000–$25,000 are becoming available in $3,000 desktop models. A general rule is that price, durability, and print quality are closely related. For example, a $400 letter-quality printer is likely to be agonizingly slow and have a short life expectancy. A $600 dot-matrix printer will be faster and more reliable, but the print quality will be inferior to that of the letter-quality machine.

The speed and durability of printers differ widely, from 15 characters per second to several hundred lines per minute. One must learn to be patient when waiting for output to be printed, tolerant of paper which bunches, and other problems.

Some printers can be equipped with *storage buffers* which allow the operator to work on one document while another is being printed.

Two forms of "feeding" paper are friction and sprocket. Friction printers allow the use of letter-quality paper, but often must be fed by hand. Sprocket feeds avoid hand feeding, but require special printer paper. The gap between the two technologies is closing, however, with letter-quality forms being placed on continuous paper, and the hole-type output coming with perforations that allow easy removal of the edge with the holes. Catalog card stock will require a vertical paper feed rather than the circular platen.

The manufacturers of printers are a different class than manufacturers of microcomputers. Microcomputer packagers usually do not make the processor, the printer, and other peripherals. Persons who sell these systems use one or a few brands, but the buyer is free to choose others, within the range of compatibility. If in doubt, the low-cost dot-matrix printer that provides medium-quality alphanumeric and graphics output should provide experience and allow a frame of reference for later purchases. Finally, a few general guidelines are helpful in selecting printers for library media applications:

1. If graphics are necessary, then a letter-quality printer will not work.
2. A dot-matrix printer is usually faster and less expensive than a letter-quality printer, but the print quality is inferior.
3. Printers must be chosen which will interface with ("speak to") the microcomputer.
4. The software purchased must support the printer chosen.
5. To ensure that the microcomputer, the printer, and the program are compatible, an in-store or onsite demonstration of the entire system is required before purchasing.
6. Letter-quality printers are both slower and more expensive than dot-matrix printers.
7. The type of feeding mechanism for regular paper, computer paper, catalog card stock, labels, and other library needs must be a factor in selection.
8. Types of ribbons (cloth or carbon), ease of changing, and price are factors to consider in the anticipated application.

Storage Devices

Secondary storage devices for the microcomputer can be classified into *tape* devices and *disk* devices, with the latter subdivided into *floppy* and *hard disk*.

Tape Storage. For most library media applications, the tape devices are unacceptable because of their lack of speed and flexibility. In fact, tapes can be dispensed with entirely in many configurations.

Disk Storage. The disk is a direct-access technology. The term *direct access* distinguishes memory from both sequential access memories (tape) and random access memories (main memory). Magnetic tape, used as a storage medium, forces the user to access the data in sequential fashion. Since this often entails going through half the tape to find a piece of data, access times are usually in minutes or (at least) tens of seconds. The length of time depends on the length of the tape and the speed of the tape recorder on which the tape is mounted.

Random access memory allows access to any location in the memory space almost instantaneously. Access time in RAM is usually measured in microseconds or nanoseconds (millionths or billionths of seconds).

Disk devices fall between random access devices and tape. Disk access time is affected by the physical position of the data record (what track it is on), and is measured in tens or hundreds of milliseconds, which is a thousand times as slow (or slower) as main-memory access, yet a thousand times faster than tape access times.

The primary distinction in disk technology for microcomputers is between floppy disks and hard disks. A second consideration is the purchase of one drive or two. Floppy disks differ from hard disks in capacity, speed of access, and cost.

''Floppies'' can usually store from 125K to 512K bytes of data. In contrast, hard disks range in the area of 10 million bytes (10 megabytes) of storage to 22 or even 40 megabytes on the more expensive work-station microcomputers. Floppies are removable, offering unlimited offline storage, while hard disks are usually nonremovable, so that the total capacity is the online capacity. Floppies utilize a moving head (read/write head) so that access time to data is slower than that of the hard disks, which have more than a single head, with either no movement (if there is one head or set of heads per track) or movement over a limited area.

A distinction should also be made between the disk itself, the storage medium, and the *disk drive,* the device used to read from and write to the disk. In a hard disk, these are packaged together, often using an enclosed technology called the *Winchester disk.* The floppy drive/disk are not packaged together. Rather, the drive is housed in the platform on which the monitor rests or in an auxiliary cabinet. Floppy disks are manually inserted and removed. A floppy disk drive may cost $500, while the disks or diskettes cost a few dollars each.

If a diskette is damaged or a hard disk experiences a ''crash,'' the data is lost. Hence, it is a good practice to *backup* the data and programs on the system. To do so conveniently usually requires the use of two disk drives, either two floppy drives or a floppy and a hard disk. While it may seem laborious to backup a hard disk containing 10 megabytes onto floppies which contain only 125K, the process is essential and not as demanding as it appears. For example, if the library media center catalog will fit on a 20 megabyte hard disk, then a system must be worked out to backup the data onto numerous floppy disks, onto a videotape, or onto a special tape system built right into the hard-disk drive.

All library media specialists are advised to have backup systems in place, no matter how large their data files are. This process may be as simple as creating duplicate copies in less than a minute to a several-hour backup process using videotape equipment. Full investigation of the various options and necessary equipment is essential. Usually the software producer will have detailed information if the required backup system is more complicated than just duplicating one floppy disk to another.

For library media applications where data files are usually very large, it would make sense to have a disk drive which would store a maximum amount of data. Unlike adding memory to a microcomputer by plugging in a card or board, the capacity of a disk is pre-set by the manufacturer. For example, an Apple II microcomputer, with a disk drive, packs 125K onto one side of a single-density disk; other microcomputers may pack data tighter into a double-density format and may use both sides of the disk simultaneously. Users should determine which type of disk their system uses so that the appropriate blank disks can be purchased. For example, buying double-sided double-density disks for the Apple is a waste of money when single-sided single-density disks are sufficient. Double-density disks have a thicker layer of oxide and may be certified for use on both sides. Hence, they are more expensive.

Data Communication

One of the most important applications for the microcomputer in the library media center is the establishment of communication by microcomputer to various local, regional, and national networks. Common uses of such equipment would be to communicate with other schools, libraries, and access databases (such as BRS or DIALOG), to participate in national networks (such as EDNET or CompuServe), or to use the services of library networks (such as OCLC, Inc.).

In order to use a *stand alone* microcomputer as an interface to a national network, one needs a *communications adapter* for the microcomputer and a telephone line. The adapter may be ''built in'' or a separate device. Its function is to convert the signals of the microcomputer into a form compatible with the telephone system. This device, known as a *modulator/demodulator (modem),* translates the signals of digital technology (computers, terminals) to those compatible with the audio signals of the telephone lines. Modems can be purchased as a separate unit or can be built into the microcomputer.

The function of the modem is to present signals in a form (analog signals) suitable for transmission across a wire, the so-called RS-232 interface. This connection usually appears on the rear of a terminal or microcomputer and is a set of 25 pins, some of which are used, some not. If one connects directly to another computer, say in the same room or an adjacent room, one can dispense with the modem; but one cannot dispense with the communications adapter or the cable that connects the adapter on one machine to those on another machine. This is popularly known as a *network* or a *local area network* (LAN).

Baud Rate, Codes, and Printers. When one begins to interface between two computers, or other pieces of equipment (e.g., a microcomputer to a line printer), one must be cognizant of the need for compatibility. One source of difficulties is in the baud rate (speed of transmitting bits) of both devices. Another is in the type of transmission, the two primary types being *asynchronous* and *synchronous* transmission.

The term *baud rate* is probably overused, the term *bit rate* being more applicable, but the idea is that if one's communication facility transmits at 300 bits per second or 1200 bits per second, the "paired" device must also be capable of communicating at that speed. The communication is usually two-way, so that both devices must be able to transmit messages and receive messages at the same speed. Many devices have selectable speeds, usually 300 bits per second (bps) or 1200 bps for telephone transmission, or 9600 bps for a hard-wired mode. In any case, one must make sure the devices are compatible; and if one already knows which computer one wishes to interface with, it is a good idea to dial up from the computer store before committing to a purchase. If one has already made a purchase and one's equipment is incompatible with a potential target machine, *protocol* adapters may be purchased to facilitate the exchange. These will, of course, increase the cost of the system, but the convenience of communication may make the expense worthwhile.

Compatibility of *codes* is another issue, similar in nature to compatibility of speeds. A code is simply a way of representing numbers, letters, and other characters in binary form (electronic signals). For example, in the ASCII code the letter *A* is represented as 1000001, the letter *B* as 1000010. The exact nature of the code is irrelevant; the *machine* has to understand it, not the microcomputer user. However, when two machines "talk to each other" they must speak the same codes (languages). Two codes have gained ascendency: IBM's EBCDIC and everyone else's ASCII. One should ascertain the code of the target machine and purchase equipment that speaks that code. Again, either hardware converters or software *conversion programs* can be purchased if necessary.

The terms *asynchronous* and *synchronous* refer to two types of transmission: a single character at a time (asynchronous) or blocks of characters (synchronous). CRT terminals are usually asynchronous. When one depresses a key on the keyboard, the corresponding character is immediately sent to the receiving computer. More expensive terminals, with storage capabilities, use the storage area (called a *buffer*) to hold the characters as typed. When one has entered a complete message, one depresses the ENTER key, and all characters (a block of characters) are sent at once. This is referred to as synchronous or *block* transmission. The main point is that "character at a time" devices are not compatible with "block at a time" transmission. One has to know the characteristics of the target machine and the characteristics of one's microcomputer—and yes, there are adapters.

In all these instances—bit rate, code, and transmission type—it is often the case that a sophisticated target machine will have a menu of selections that it can "understand," making it easier for a variety of terminals, microcomputers, and other devices to interface with it.

The *parity bit* is an error-detection mechanism that is sometimes used, sometimes not used, by computer and data communications equipment. It consists of an extra bit that is added as necessary to make the total number of 1 bits even or odd. For example, in even parity the ASCII character for the letter A (1000001) would be "o.k.," since it already has 2 ones, which is an even number of ones. Hence, the parity bit would be set to zero:

$$10000010_1 \text{ (Two 1s are o.k.)}$$
$$\text{parity}$$

The ASCII code for C (1000011) has 3 ones, which is not even. The parity bit would be set to a 1, raising the total number of 1s to four, which is even, hence fine and dandy.

$$10000111_1 \text{ (Four 1s are o.k.)}$$
$$\text{parity}$$

The function of the parity bit can be seen by considering an error in transmission. Say that the letter C has been transmitted (with even parity):

$$\text{sent: } 10000111$$

and the second bit from the left is garbled in transmission, now being received as a 1 (due to "noise" on the line):

$$\text{received: } 11000111$$

The receiving device knows that an error occurred because there are five 1s (odd), and even parity is being used. The receiving device cannot correct the error in this scheme, but it can ask for retransmission.

The point is not the error-detection capabilities of the parity bit, but the fact that some devices use even parity, some odd, some none at all. What parity is used, if any, is irrelevant to the end user, except that the two machines must be compatible. The type of parity is usually selectable on a device, so that most devices can be made compatible (without an adapter, thank goodness). There are switches, called *dip switches,* that must be set to the desired parity type.

The world of interfacing equipment is fraught with frustration. There are *so* many options, and (surprisingly or not) even the computer center operators, programmers, and management at the target computer may not know, or be able to find out readily, what settings are compatible. As mentioned earlier, if one already has access to a target computer, phone in from the microcomputer store. If it works, fine; if not, have the salespeople attempt to achieve compatibility.

If one does not have a specific target computer in mind, choose standard options, such as an ASCII terminal, and transmission at 300 and 1200 baud (faster is better, but not always compatible). There are two protocols at 1200 baud, in asynchronous mode, and this will interface with most of the world. Adapters can be purchased as needed when interfacing with devices outside this range of capabilities.

Maintenance

A major question when one purchases microcomputer equipment is its maintenance and repair. Several methods of maintenance are available, differing in cost and convenience and speed of service. In the most convenient type of maintenance contract, the technical people come to one's site. However, this type of contract is usually expensive, costing as much per year as a quarter of the cost of the entire system if done "on call" or at high "per visit" rates. It is a necessary cost with large systems that are not easily moved, but is probably excessive for a microcomputer system. Hence, one is usually forced to choose between carrying the device back to the store for service or shipping it to some out-of-town location. Local facilities are far preferable to a ship-back system, and one of the reasons for dealing with standard equipment.

In any case, the question of types of maintenance contracts and their respective costs should be addressed before a purchase is made, and every endeavor made to have maintenance as close to home as possible. This will minimize downtime of the system.

Other Considerations

Sooner or later in the microcomputer purchase decision, the questions of language and operating systems will arise, particularly if the decision involves a brand such as IBM or one of its clones. Since so many versions of BASIC and other computer languages are installed on popular microcomputers, the major issue is whether a particular software package will work on a particular machine. At the time of purchase of either software or hardware, the library media specialist must inquire if the microcomputer can handle a particular software application. A demonstration at the time of purchase, or direct knowledge received from another library media specialist who is using the product, is essential to ensure compatibility of software and hardware.

In the short history of microcomputer hardware, many changes have been made in languages and operating systems. The *operating system* refers to the internal governing system through which the microcomputer controls the disk drives and other peripherals. The *language* is the coded instruction which the microcomputer uses to carry out its work. Many versions of BASIC and Pascal languages are available, and there does not seem to be any trend toward a universal computer language such as one finds in printed music. Differing operating systems exist, such as CP/M, MSDOS, ProDOS, and UNIX. Some claim that one of these will predominate, but it is too early to tell.

The best advice seems to be to get the intended application(s) up and running at purchase time, before ordering any product. Try to stay with a popular version of a computer language and a popular operating system. If one is certain that a microcomputer and a particular program will be paired and in operation for a number of years, then language and operating system are not as important. For example, if a circulation system is installed and the microcomputer will be used for nothing except circulation, as long as all components of the system operate smoothly, other considerations are of less importance. Trying to see into the future and guess what is ahead is just that—a guess.

Should the library media specialist buy a clone of a popular microcomputer? Many companies try to duplicate machines sold by other manufacturers, such as Apple or IBM, claiming near-compatibility. At times, the market becomes a mass of confusion with claims and counterclaims. While there is no one answer to whether a clone will serve as well as the original brand, the library media specialist should make absolutely certain that the software advertised for the popular brand will actually work on the cloned machine. Very slight incompatibility can be disastrous, and often there is no one to ask for help, unless that is a part of an agreement made with either software producer or hardware vendor.

A final question concerns obsolescence. At what point should a library media specialist invest in a microcomputer system? It is impossible to buy a microcomputer today which will be an industry-wide model for the foreseeable future. Whatever the library media specialist buys will be obsolete at the time it is unpacked from its crate. Therefore, obsolescence is not a major factor in buying a microcomputer.

If a microcomputer is purchased and performs a particular function well over a five- to ten-year period, then that is what the library media specialist needs. The market will change and grow, but the outmoded microcomputer can perform a task faithfully until a replacement system is selected.

The Facility Concept of the Microcomputer Classroom or Laboratory

John Griffiths and Deborah Hetrick

As a school begins to acquire microcomputers, two questions arise: Where will the microcomputers be located? And who will manage them? A variety of answers to these questions are demonstrated in schools across the nation; however, sooner or later, the library media center staff will serve (*is* serving) as the most satisfactory answer. Library media specialists have gained unique experience over the last twenty years in acquiring, disseminating, maintaining, and seeing that all types of audiovisual equipment are kept in good repair. Adding microcomputers to the array is a logical step in most schools.

Many of the principles of managing audiovisual equipment and materials apply to managing microcomputer equipment and software. Dust, an enemy of all camera lenses, tape recorders, and 16mm projectors, is a more acute problem with microcomputers. However, some unique problems with the microcomputer deserve careful attention. For example, it requires a steady and unaltered power supply if it is to function properly. A single surge of electricity can destroy the microprocessor and the RAM and ROM chips, rendering the entire machine inoperable.

Four configurations of microcomputer facilities are emerging in schools today. In the first, the school owns a few microcomputers which are either centralized, spread among the classrooms, or moved about as needed. In the second, a computer laboratory is set up and teachers may schedule it for whole-class, small-group, or individual use. The third scenario has several computer laboratories, each dedicated to a particular type of computer application and available by reservation. In the final stage, the introduction of computers into classrooms will find microcomputers as conveniently located as the pencil sharpener.

School library media specialists know that there are basically two options in managing technology: one may manage either equipment or people. Equipment may be moved to people, when and where they need it, on a temporary basis; or it may be placed in a fixed location for students and teachers. In the latter case, people will move to the machines.

Few Available Microcomputers

In some situations, one microcomputer is purchased for a school building. It may be placed in the library media center or it may be assigned to one particular classroom. If one or more microcomputers are available, they may be placed on portable carts and moved from the library media center to classrooms, as one does the 16mm projector. Such "dividing" of microcomputers is not practical if the goal is a systematic impact on a curricular area. However, it may be the best "political" decision in the beginning stages of microcomputer program development.

If a system of portable microcomputers is chosen, a rolling cart that will handle both microcomputer and peripherals, and will permit use *on the cart* (rather than having it moved to a desk or table in the classroom), is essential. Such constant moving is not wise, however, for connections and cords are vulnerable to wear and breaking. Portable units are most vulnerable to power supply irregularities, since it is not feasible to install "dedicated" power outlets at all user locations. Carts for roving computers should be equipped with grounded, three-prong cords and power-supply-protection devices. A protected outlet should be installed on the cart for each power cord on the computer. A system with a computer, monitor, printer, and telephone modem may require four protected outlets for complete reliability.

Portable systems should be secured to their carts and provided with dust covers. Portable units can also be fitted with carrying cases, which are especially useful for take-home computers.

Computer carts should be the regular audiovisual type, with large rubber tires to reduce shock and bumps. They should also have shelving for supplies and accessories. Most microcomputer systems appropriate for school use are not designed for easy carrying, yet carrying microcomputers *without* cases or carts increases the danger of damage. (Small, portable, self-contained units are available, but are not typically compatible with school uses because little good educational software has been developed for them.) Keyboard computers, with television-signal output, can be hooked directly to home televisions; but computers with RGB (red, green, blue) or video output need monitors or modulator/converters for use with home televisions. Some newer model televisions are equipped for direct computer video input.

Management of this system will be similar to that of portable video equipment. Such equipment, however, is usually requested for a somewhat longer period of time than the 16mm or the filmstrip projector. The systems have more component parts, and some cautions are necessary for teachers and students if the equipment is to be handled as carefully as necessary. For ease of management and reduced maintenance problems, the microcomputer laboratory is more practical in many ways. For this reason, the planning process (which follows) reflects this *preferred* configuration. Moreover, the process may be applied to the first purchase of a microcomputer for the school library media center.

Setting Up the Computer Laboratory

If the computing facility is to be consolidated into a central laboratory that may be scheduled or requisitioned by teachers, a number of major considerations are essential. Few school library media centers have enough space for the microcomputers. However, if a classroom is to be remodeled, this location should be close to the media center, to ease the management of the laboratory.

Planning a laboratory and observing the kind of teaching which takes place in it will help, should the microcomputer be merged into classrooms at a later time. Indeed, the constantly reduced costs of hardware shows promise of providing microcomputers in schools in greater numbers in the near future. Thus, the microcomputer laboratory should be considered a *temporary* solution, until technology changes and microcomputers become even more widely available.

Phase 1. Planning. The first step is to list the types of computing which should be taught in the laboratory, such as computer-assisted instruction, programming, word processing, and networking. This entails a projection of all teaching or curriculum requirements and the related software. While the choice of both determines hardware requirements, the following hardware specifications are determined by software characteristics:

Minimum memory size
Mass (disk) storage capacity
Display (screen) size, resolution, and color
Keyboard and other input devices (scanners, paddles, etc.)
Communications for local and line uses
Printers and plotters
Operating system software

Curriculum requirements also determine facility housekeeping, operation and scheduling, usage policies and procedures, and materials storage. School library media specialists must keep in mind that teaching, curriculum, and software requirements determine user training needs, as well as location of laboratory and provision of hardware.

Curriculum requirements, rather than software specifications, indicate how many microcomputers are necessary. Fundamentally, the number of microcomputers depends upon the number of students or users, a number expressed in *user hours* and compared to the number of hours that microcomputers are available. For example, one microcomputer, in use 6 hours per day each week, is available for 1,080 hours maximum use during a 36-week year. If a school has 1,080 students, each student would get 1 hour each on the machine in a year. Ten machines would provide 10 hours for each student.

Hands-on time, except for that used to teach programming, is determined by the software, or by the amount of time it takes to run a program or a lesson. The time to run a program is further determined by the hardware; for example, a cassette program takes longer to load into the microcomputer than does a disk program. If a reading program has 30 lessons in it, and each lesson takes 20 to 30 minutes, then one student, working alone, will take 10 to 15 hours to complete the package (exclusive of loading into the microcomputer). A reading class with 20 students and one computer will need 40 to 60 weeks to complete the package. Ten computers would allow the class to complete the program in 6 weeks.

Once the type, capacity, and number of microcomputers are known, additional hardware requirements can be identified again, based upon the curriculum to be implemented. These requirements typically include specifications for printers, communication modems, and accessories such as network controllers, hard disks, and game paddles. Again, software requirements help determine just what peripheral devices and accessories are required.

The number and type of printers depend upon the type of printed output required. For example, word processing packages, which can be used for preparing tests, papers, and reports, usually require printers capable of producing both draft- and letter-quality printing (e.g., dot matrix and daisywheel). At the present time, dot-matrix printers are still distinguishable from daisywheel copies. One printer is probably necessary for each microcomputer used for word processing. If the printer is dedicated for student papers, a high-quality dot matrix should suffice; however, if the library media specialist wishes to send correspondence, a letter-quality printer may be preferable. Computers used for teaching programming should have printers for producing program listings, but a dot-matrix printer is sufficient for this use.

It is, of course, ideal to have a printer attached to each computer, but the cost of such systems often prohibits this configuration. Accessory network controllers can be used to make one printer serve up to 32 computers.

Hard-disk drives can be added to networks to provide disk storage for computers, which would therefore not need to be equipped with individual disk drives. Use of a network restricts the distance at which computers can be placed from the controller. Networks are impractical if portability is required or if users require microcomputers at specific locations.

A formal cost analysis should be prepared for purchase of an entire system. This helps in deciding between microcomputers with comparable capabilities, before the final budget is prepared. Two types of costs are identified: one-time costs, associated with equipment acquisition, and recurring costs, associated with equipment operation and use.

One-time costs include purchase costs, which should also include delivery and set-up costs, installation costs for preparing space, and training costs. Recurring costs include maintenance costs, utilities and insurance, subscriptions, and supplies. One-time and recurring costs can vary from vendor to vendor and can be the basis for choosing between vendors.

Sufficient documentation and manuals must be acquired to accompany each microcomputer, peripheral device, accessory, and software package. These manuals are not always provided with the purchase of equipment, and often are a hidden expense.

Additional factors to be considered in acquiring hardware include compatibility, expandability, ease of use, and vendor reputation. Microcomputer hardware configurations can take many different forms, depending upon their planned uses. Library media specialists may select all one brand or from different manufacturers. A facility can be designed as a number of individual workstations, each with a different type of keyboard-computer, a one-channel–one-color television receiver, and disk drive. A facility with a variety of hardware and configurations, some perhaps with printers and some with telephone modems, allows more flexibility and helps to reduce specific hardware dependency. This arrangement, however, is not compatible with classroom style group instruction and teacher interaction and increases the difficulty of teaching beginning users.

Compatibility refers to the degree to which different microcomputers and devices can be connected together. For example, hard-disk-based networks often allow different brands and models of computers to be connected. Simple communication networks, such as Radio Shack's, require complete compatibility among connected units. Printers which work on one type of computer usually do not work on other types.

The easiest way to assess compatibility is to determine what standards are met by different computers and devices. Standards are stated in terms of *interfaces.* Printers, for example, require either serial or parallel interfaces, which are mutually incompatible. Telephone communication modems typically require what are called RS232 interfaces. Some computers, such as Radio Shack's Model III, can be ordered with RS232 interfaces; other computers require an add-on interface, which must be purchased as an accessory and installed by the owner. Hard-disk networks require compatible interfaces on all interconnected units.

Expandability refers to the degree to which individual computer capabilities can be increased by adding components, such as plug-in memory boards and interfaces. An Apple computer with one disk drive will accommodate an additional disk drive, simply by being plugged in; more drives will require the installation of an additional plug-in interface board. Expandability is important so that a microcomputer installation will meet your current needs, yet have the ability to expand to meet future requirements.

Ease of use refers to the degree with which users may operate systems without supervision or assistance. This affects the type of training and the amount of supervision that must be provided. School library media specialists traditionally have provided both media-use and equipment-use workshops for teachers who did not have these experiences in their teacher preparation programs. Each year, students are given inservice training in using the media and other audiovisual equipment. Because the library media staff is unlikely to be expanded with the addition of this new technology, systems that are easy to use will be necessary—or media staffs will find themselves spending too much time with microcomputers and neglecting the other forms of information which students and teachers need and which are available in the media center.

School library media specialists are also aware of the need to ascertain *vendor reputation* in purchasing hardware of all types. Microcomputer hardware and software are not exceptions to this rule. However, this new technology has developed a totally new group of vendors, rather than selling its hardware in the showrooms of traditional suppliers of audiovisual equipment. Vendor reputation may be assessed initially by the number of people who have purchased from a particular vendor or dealer: the more satisfied the customers, the more reputable the vendor. A more reliable approach is to talk to people who already own the particular hardware being considered, who can answer questions about reliability, maintenance, ease of use, and satisfaction. Promptness and satisfaction are especially important when it comes to service and maintenance.

At this point, the total cost of software, hardware, and accessories can be calculated and the acquisition budget prepared. Equipment should not be ordered, however, until the installation plan has been determined to be feasible. If the facility will not accommodate the proposed equipment, another facility should be considered or the equipment list should be pared.

Equipment buyers should take advantage of the substantial educational discounts available from most vendors. Some states and local districts have negotiated *blank purchase orders* or *buy plans* under which schools can purchase equipment at large discounts, as much as 50 percent. Most vendors offer educational discounts of 20 percent for individual purchasers.

Phase 2. The Installation. The objective of the installation phase is to design the laboratory layout and determine power supply, furnishings, security, and storage, as well as the test and acceptance requirements. Microcomputers depend upon a stable power supply. As mentioned previously, power surges and interruptions can damage circuits and cause data loss on disks and tapes that are in use during power-supply interruptions. The best idea is to install dedicated electrical circuits with sufficient grounded outlets. This is a challenge in most buildings which were not built to accommodate technology of any type. Also, it is necessary to plan to have electricity available—not just in the wall, but wherever computers will be positioned in the lab. This may require power strips, overhead pulldown extensions, or other reliable connections.

A single 30-ampere circuit will support up to 15 systems. Grounded extension cords and outlets help reduce static electricity, which can cause malfunctions and data loss. Static can also be reduced with anti-static carpeting and sprays.

The microcomputer laboratory may be used to connect students with outside facilities. Telephone lines for computer communications should be free from operator and switchboard interruptions, since such interruptions will break communication links and may cause loss of data.

Adequate working space must be provided for each computer system. Working space should be easily accessible, comfortable, free from distracting noise or light, and readily visible from the supervisor's desk. For safety, cables and wires should be "secured"—out of the way of users' feet and chairs. Individual workstations take up to 40 square feet of space, including microcomputer space, workspace, seating, and access room. Printers and additional monitors take more space. Work surfaces should be 25 to 28 inches high, for adult-user comfort. For younger users, worksurface heights should allow comfortable keyboard operation, while seated, with hands just lower than elbows, elbows at the user's side.

Classroom activity tables, rather than ordinary writing tables, may be the appropriate height for comfortable computer use. Most ordinary tables, however, come in 29- and 30-inch heights, but can be modified by shortening their legs. Modification is cheaper than purchasing custom-made furniture, although special-purpose microcomputer furniture is becoming available at reasonable prices. Ordinary chairs may be used with 25- to 28-inch-high tables.

Overhead lighting does not usually produce distracting reflections or glare on microcomputer monitor screens, but windows do. Curtains or blinds eliminate glare and reflections from bright windows.

Microcomputers must be physically secure. They must be protected from abuse, theft, and unauthorized use. Supervised locations are most secure and additional measures are usually not needed. Unsupervised and portable units should be bolted to tables or carts. Take-home microcomputers should be checked out only to responsible, trained users. Damage to loaned microcomputers should be covered by general school equipment policies.

If microcomputer software is to be in the media center and the laboratory is not directly accessible, programs will be checked out and taken to the laboratory. Library media centers with electromagnetic inventory-control equipment will be able to protect documents and equipment, but magnetic strips or other detection devices should not be placed on software programs since tapes and disks are sensitive to magnetic interference. Until microcomputer software collections become much larger, it may be that software programs initially should be shelved and controlled as if they were reference or reserved materials. This will help ensure that programs are available at school when students need them. Microcomputer programs should not require the same two-week or indefinite loan periods as are given to other media center materials. Most programs are of short duration.

When software programs are delivered after purchase, they should be inspected to see that all documentation is included. Warranty cards must be returned to supplier to confirm purchase in case documentation is lost or to ask for replacement programs. A decision must also be made either to store programs in the box or notebook supplied by the producer or to purchase uniform storage containers. Dust-proof storage for software must be provided.

Shelving for how-to-use-the-microcomputer manuals and system software documentation should be near the microcomputers. Software is packaged in many sizes and formats, so adjustable shelving is most convenient.

Two backup tapes and/or disks should be acquired, or permission should be secured for making copies for each program-original so that the collection contains the original, one working copy, and one backup copy for each program. This method of purchasing and/or creating two generations of copies ensures that the original magnetic media is kept free from handling damage and from wear caused by repeated use. The backup copy is used to create new working copies as necessary, and the original is used if both the working and backup copies are damaged. Working copies of tapes and disks should be shelved with program documentation. Backup copies should be filed separately, and the original copies of all program tapes and disks should be stored away from the laboratory.

Before renovation starts, a layout chart should be prepared to ensure that the space will be arranged properly. The layout chart is a map of the facility, and it shows the locations of microcomputers, tables, shelves, desks, and other equipment. Specific arrangement of microcomputers in a facility is determined by their planned uses. Group instruction will require classroom-style layout, with a large monitor at the teacher's desk. Arrangements for individual workstations can be a variety of configurations, such as clustered or along the walls. Each workstation can be set up to operate independently, or they can share peripherals such as printers and hard disks. The layout will determine the location of all electrical power outlets and telephone connections, and will show how network and power cables must be routed. Microcomputers usually have 6-foot (sometimes 8-foot) power cables; so if they are to be located more than 6 feet from power outlets, grounded extension cables will have to be installed.

Once the layout plan is known to be feasible—that is, the space is available and can be renovated to suit—delivery can be scheduled. The approximate date by which the space can be ready is determined, and an additional 72 hours should be allowed ''to let the dust settle.'' Equipment is ordered for delivery immediately following that date.

Testing and acceptance procedures should be followed. Identify the person responsible for unpacking equipment and setting it up. In some cases this will be the salesperson; in others it may be left to the media center staff.

As soon as the equipment is set up and connected, the installation test is conducted. All equipment is checked to verify that it works as expected. All equipment must respond to controls and commands as described in the user manuals. It is important to check all equipment thoroughly. Defective units should be repacked and returned to the supplier. In addition, all warranty cards should be filled out and serial numbers recorded in equipment inventories.

All equipment should be left turned on for 24 hours following the installation test, and then turned off. At this point, the acceptance test is conducted. This test repeats the installation test, after which malfunctioning equipment is repacked and returned.

The installation and acceptance test sequence assures that all equipment works as expected and that it will continue to do so. Microcomputers are now so reliable that if problems do not appear in the first 24 hours, the equipment is probably problem-free. For payment purposes, no equipment should be considered "delivered" until the installation and acceptance tests have been completed.

Phase 3. Maintenance. The maintenance phase follows installation. During this phase, the library media specialist ensures that equipment operates correctly and is reliable. Warranties cover equipment failure for various periods after installation. *Basic* warranties cover from 30 days to 6 months, depending upon the equipment. *Extended* warranties may be purchased to cover equipment failures for 6 to 12 months, but may be too expensive. Warranty coverage usually includes parts and labor, but may not include the costs of onsite service. Check with the supplier or dealer to be sure these arrangements are clear at the time equipment is ordered.

Service or maintenance agreements may be purchased for an annual cost range from 10 to 20 percent of the original equipment costs, and may be the most cost-effective approach to maintenance. Service agreements usually cover costs of repairs and service. Warranties and service agreements usually do not cover the costs of damage to software—for example, if a disk drive damages a disk.

Warranty and service agreement plans are best implemented through one person who "tracks" the performance of the equipment. If the library media center has limited staff, this may be assigned to an interested student or faculty member who will serve as hardware or technical coordinator. The process is not a difficult one, but it must be done. Ideally, every piece of equipment is tested at least monthly to make sure it is working correctly. In most situations, however, problems occur when the equipment is needed most. The hardware or technical coordinator is responsible for notifying the library media specialist of problems. At this time the service agency must be called, the repair work verified, and the equipment tested to see if the repair solved the problem. The technical coordinator is also responsible for periodical preventive maintenance, such as cleaning disk-drive heads with cleaning disks and adjusting disk-drive speed. Print wheels and printer ribbons must also be maintained.

The school library media specialist must secure the efforts of all teachers and students who use the microcomputer lab to help in caring for the equipment. Eating, drinking, chewing gum, combing hair, and dropping objects into the keyboards must be prohibited. Although the effect of chalkboard dust upon microcomputer floppy disks is not yet clear, it is safe to assume it is harmful, and it is best to keep as much distance as possible between chalkboards and equipment. Dry marker boards also create dust; so newsprint pads and markers may be effective substitutes. This equipment is perhaps more fragile than most other audiovisual equipment, except perhaps the video camera, recorders, and monitors. Students and teachers will enjoy using the equipment, but attention must be directed to the problems which simple misuse may cause.

Phase 4. Operations. This phase is concerned with day-to-day operations, management of the facility, and operating budget items. Operating budget items consist of recurring expenses associated with microcomputer use, usually supplies, subscriptions, telephone and utility costs, and insurance. Maintenance or service agreement costs are also operating budget items.

Supplies, or ''consumables,'' consist of paper, printer wheels and ribbons, disks and tapes, and adhesive labels. Paper must be provided for each printer, and the type of paper is determined by the type of printer and the uses made of the printing capability. Most printers require *continuous paper,* either in rolls or fanfolded boxes. Printers may require pin-feed paper with sprocket holes along the sides. Some printers may adjust to various widths of paper, and appropriate sizes must be stocked. Printers used primarily for word processing may require ordinary sheets of bond paper; others may use bond-quality continuous paper with tear-off sprocket-hole edges. Attention must be paid to printer specifications, which state what weight of paper to use. Some small, light-duty printers require special heat or impact-sensitive paper. The additional cost of this paper is offset by the fact that such printers do not require ribbons.

Replacement cartridges for both dot-matrix and daisywheel printer ribbons must be purchased. Daisywheel printers have replaceable print wheels which are available in a variety of typefaces. Plastic print wheels are fragile and spares must be kept.

Good-quality blank disks and tapes are necessary for creating backups of packages, for storing users' programs and data, and for supporting recordkeeping packages. It may be that they could be sold in the school's bookstore; otherwise, the library media specialist may choose to supply disks at cost, if they are not considered part of the supplies provided for students.

Tapes for microcomputer use must be ''leaderless'' and no longer than 60-

minute size, since the thinner tape in longer sizes does not wear well. Disks should be single- or double-sided and single or double density, as required by the disk drives. Adhesive labels for individual tapes and disks are necessary.

It is useful to have ordinary graph paper available for microcomputers since it allows easy preparation of designs and programs. The cost of paper is such that, again, students who make extensive use of it may be required to purchase some of the paper they use.

Phase 5. Use and Control. The purpose of this phase is to define facility staffing needs, operating schedules, access and usage policies, and usage procedures. A staff person should be present at all times when the facility is open. This person should be responsible for monitoring users, checking software in and out, and answering simple questions about equipment operation. If the facility is to be used for group instruction, an instructor and an additional assistant should be present. An optimum number is 1 assistant for every 6 to 8 microcomputers used for instruction.

It is obvious that administrators are not able to add extensive staff to the microcomputer program. Library media specialists may do well to consider library technicians or aides to help. In media centers that use students as assistants, many will be able to assist in many monitoring functions. Certainly the microcomputer laboratory will be a preferred work location.

If the facility is to be operated on a classroom schedule, access should be strictly restricted to members of scheduled classes. In such classes, student hands-on time will be scheduled according to the instructional requirements. If the facility is to be operated as a resource center, before or after classes or during study hall, then an equal-access policy must be developed.

Facility monitors should also ensure that consistent operating procedures are used with equipment. Ideally, only those users who have been trained in the facility should be permitted to use it. In practice, with many users owning their computers, it may be difficult to ensure consistency. Brief orientation and procedure training sessions should be offered to new, but experienced, users.

Monitors should attempt to make sure that software is not damaged, stolen, or copied without permission. Stringent circulation procedures will ensure that software is accounted for, and that damaged software is immediately identified. Since damage can occur through mishandling disks or through tampering, it is important to identify users who need more training or closer supervision.

Beyond One Laboratory

Building multiple microcomputer laboratories in a school allows specialized functions to occur more easily. One lab might be established to handle programming classes, another to handle the use of instructional packages. Another lab might be available for business applications such as word processing, spreadsheets, and database management, while another might be equipped to offer graphics and design creations. Each lab would need different equipment and peripherals, a different layout, and different supervision. Some schools no longer teach typewriting and have replaced their typewriters with microcomputers. Such a change requires less adaptation because electrical power is already in place, and the typing room is already suitable for one machine per student.

In schools where multiple laboratories are proposed, plans might include assigning some machines to specific tasks and placing these machines permanently in departments. A few microcomputers should remain portable to allow for demonstration or teaching in any area of the school. Microcomputers equipped to monitor scientific experiments, connected into synthesizers and large speakers, interfaced with videodisk machines, and connected to graphics tablets are best dedicated to a particular task and should be supervised by the appropriate teacher. In these cases, control for technical matters such as security, maintenance and repair, software evaluation, and software purchases may nevertheless be centralized.

In 1986, a few schools boasted of having one microcomputer for each student. These schools had a specialized staff, including designers, inservice trainers, software maintenance personnel, and a technical staff. While these schools may stress traditional instruction, teachers are experimenting with large-scale course applications on microcomputers. Most of the students' drill and practice, and their writing assignments, are accomplished on machines rather than paper. Networking within each classroom, plus a master teaching station, allows the teacher to monitor and communicate with each student. The teacher station in this situation might be equipped with a screen large enough to be seen by the entire class (measuring 4 or 5 feet diagonally), a hard disk for storage of programs, and full network capabilities.

While this was not the typical school, the possibilities of full microcomputer use are in the not-so-distant future, and all school library media specialists should be planning for this level of microcomputer technology in their schools.

Microcomputers in an Elementary School

Arly Gunderman

New developments within the microcomputer industry and the steadily decreasing cost of the equipment have given parents the ability to purchase microcomputer systems for the home. The same declining cost has also given educators the opportunity to provide at least an introductory experience with high technology in all schools, in large and small districts, and in lower-funded school corporations as well as affluent systems.

It has become a primary responsibility of all educators to help determine the best experiences for children to have with this new form of technology. As with all other phases of the education process, the bases for decisions for implementation of a microcomputer program in the schools must be grounded in educational theory, and the microcomputer program must be integrated within the established curriculum. This integration may include learning through ''intrinsically motivating'' games which was the subject of a recent study. The final paragraph states:

> The new technology of computers—with its uniquely rich possibilities for responsive fantasy, captivating sensory effects, and individual adaptability—has an unprecedented potential for creating fascinating educational environments. But as our cultural experience with television indicates, great potential does not guarantee wise use. I have tried to point the way, in this report, toward a humane and productive use of this new educational technology that avoids the dangers of soulless drudgery on the one hand and mind-numbing entertainment on the other.[1]

In 1978, Pike Lake School's administration, staff, teachers, media specialist, and parents began to meet the microcomputer challenge.

---

[1]Thomas W. Malone, ''What Makes Things Fun to Learn? A Study of Intrinsically Motivating Computer Games.'' Palo Alto, Calif.: Xerox Research Center, August 1984), p. 82.

54

Implementation

Microcomputers are considered essential at Pike Lake School. In six years, the media center went from one microcomputer through one-by-one additions until it reached a total of 25 in 1986. The arrival of the microcomputer was a second step in computer literacy at Pike Lake. Introductions to the possibilities of computer programs were given to students (most often fourth, fifth, and sixth graders) and teachers through the MECC timesharing terminals connected to a large computer network in Minneapolis. Terminals were placed in the media center and scheduling was done by the school library media specialist.

Microcomputers were placed in this central location for several reasons. The size of the media center at Pike Lake made the choice somewhat easier, perhaps, than in another situation, where the facilities are not nearly so spacious. This ''room'' has 6,500 square feet in the center of the building, for it is a former court-yard which was covered. However, placement of terminals and, later, microcomputers in this room was a logical choice for several additional reasons.

The school library media specialist, already actively choosing both print and media materials to supplement the curriculum, could add them to the bibliographies for appropriate curriculum units. Providing teachers with excellent software from which to choose is also a function of the media specialist in this building. The placement of the microcomputer in the school library media center allows for the addition of microcomputer software to other forms of audiovisual media which are integrated into the curriculum of the school. It is easier for the teacher to find all the available materials on a given topic if they are housed in one central location.

The school library media specialist also assisted in implementing a wide variety of activities with microcomputers. It was easier to determine how, when, and to whom computer literacy training was being given. Beginning with kindergarten students, a planned sequence of activities is given so that students are familiar with the microcomputer and are able to use it with ease when classes come to the media center. Placing the school's microcomputers in one location permits access by a total class as well as individual students, rather than restricting computer use to one or two students in a single classroom for a very limited period of time.

The management of classroom-related use of the microcomputers is simplified when they are in one location and easily accessible by all students. All students (grades 1 through 5) at Pike Lake are scheduled twice a week into the media center. Subjects include math, reading, and language arts. Since it is important that someone be available to monitor use of the microcomputers, an aide in the media center is assigned to the computer area to assist students. When an entire class comes, the teacher may help; and the library media specialist is available when no classes use the media center, as well as when the unit is part of a media center lesson.

Uses

Since all microcomputers are placed in a central location which is open to students at all times of day, they may be accessed without disturbing a classroom or a teacher who may have been assigned responsibility for one or more microcomputers in that classroom. Teachers who have been asked to take responsibility for the first microcomputer placed in that building tend to establish or assume territorial imperatives which are difficult to modify later. The scheduling of microcomputers through a ''disinterested'' party can also assist in equitable sharing of these sought-after machines.

An educator's first concern is with the effect of any new technology on instruction. A major curricular use of the computer was in the area of recordkeeping for individualized instruction programs. Individualized programs have always required the establishment of a recordkeeping and monitoring system. For a system developed at the Reeder Elementary School in Mounds View, Minnesota, in the early 1970s, this recordkeeping was done on the district computer.[2] Such records may now be maintained on a microcomputer.

Perhaps one of the more exciting possibilities for computer-assisted instruction is in special education. The potential for use with the child with special learning problems has scarcely been touched. An article described the program in one Educational Cooperative Service Unit (ECSU) in Minnesota:

> The West Central ECSU . . . had the opportunity to modify and adapt software and hardware for special education students, especially the physically handicapped. Software modifications were made at the direct request of special education teachers in area schools. For example, a teacher may have seen a computer program being used in a regular classroom and felt that there was a physically or mentally handicapped student who could benefit from that program, though not in its present form. The ECSU staff made modifications so it would be usable for that student and for students with similar problems. New materials requested by teachers are developed as time permits. Most modifications were made on MECC [Minnesota Educational Computer Consortium] courseware.[3]

The school library media specialist uses the microcomputer for storing information about resources in the Pike Lake Media Center. The ease of maintaining bibliographies of materials by subject or grade levels, as well as circulation and overdue writing, can save the time of the clerical staff.

Many time-saving applications have been found by using the microcomputer in this elementary school. In many instances these time-saving applications reduce

---

[2]Reeder Elementary School Staff, ''Reeder School Makes the Computer Work for Individuality,'' *Minnesota Elementary School Principal* 15 (March 1973): 4–6.

[3]Gene Jurgens, ''Spotlight on Microcomputers and Special Education,'' *Minnesota Elementary School Principal* 25 (Winter 1983): 13.

the clerical tasks of the person using the program, and permit all school staff to work with students rather than grading worksheets or locating overdue books or other repetitive tasks which, while necessary, do not directly help children.

Managing Microcomputers

As stated earlier, microcomputers are considered essential at Pike Lake Elementary School. Placement in the elementary library has proved to be an effective management practice. It is always more efficient to assign the management of all equipment to a single person. This person can then take responsibility for the circulation of equipment to teachers and students (and the microcomputers at Pike Lake *do* go home over the weekend and on holidays) and the methods of scheduling students into the center.

Finally, responsibility for the choices of the best software to fit the particular curriculum need are given to someone who is well aware of the total instructional resources of the school, and thereby helping choose the best media for the learning situation, at the same time reducing the chance of unnecessary duplication or selection of inferior computer software.

Placing the microcomputer program under the library media specialist has been very effective, and this pattern of organization has received support from both teachers and students.

PART TWO

OPERATING THE FACILITY

In recent years, budgets for school library media centers have remained the same or have decreased. Inflation has further eroded spending power, and many services have been eliminated or reduced as a result. School library media specialists are making many changes in an effort to continue needed services. New ways to accomplish old tasks may help accomplish this.

In addition to new ways to accomplish old tasks, some new tasks may be initiated. This is not without pitfalls. The school library media specialist must overcome the urge to *automate* tasks when they are better done *manually*—such as placing an audiovisual supply inventory on the microcomputer. This may mean going from the supply room to the microcomputer to another location to subtract two overhead projector bulbs, when a clipboard record in the supply room would be handier, just as efficient, and faster.

One of the greatest challenges facing a library media specialist is to manage the center's warehousing operations. Circulation routines, technical service operations, and reporting can take inordinate proportions of the library media specialist's time, with seemingly little reward. Warehousing and management duties are vital if the library media center is to function effectively, but most of the time there are too few staff to carry out repetitive tasks.

Managing with software offers one solution. Loertscher describes administrative uses of the microcomputer. Chase and Klasing describe the process of using word processing, database management programs, spreadsheets, and integrated systems.

Because demands imposed on the media center may require rapid response, communication by electronic mail will improve service. If media specialists weigh the benefits of using the microcomputer to help manage, they will learn that electronic mail can be cost effective. Epler's article is devoted to showing these advantages. Part 2 describes an automated workplace for the library media specialist and points to the mastery needed at each point of entry.

Administrative Uses

David V. Loertscher

Library media specialists are constantly pressured to perform more and varied services, which puts a great deal of emphasis on the storage or "warehouse" functions. These functions demand a major amount of time and effort just to keep the library media center operational. Shelving, equipment delivery, circulation routines, magazine storage and retrieval, as well as numbers of other mundane tasks, take the primary attention when more professional tasks should be under way.

One solution posed in the literature is to seek every means to streamline or automate clerical routines so that the library media specialist can spend a significant portion of time with students and teachers. With the advent of the microcomputer, new hopes for greater efficiency with time-saving routines have surfaced.

All library media specialists would like a microcomputer which would handle all cataloging problems, circulation headaches, "overdue woes," scheduling hassles, reporting drudgery, and all other nonprofessional tasks—as if by magic. To hear some advocates speak of microcomputers, one merely punches a button and everything just happens. It is not that simple. Computerized management of library media operations takes more careful planning than instructional applications because the programs are longer and more complex than most instruction modules. Also, microcomputers cannot only assist with media center operations, but can create bigger problems than they were designed to alleviate. They can make a task easier, or more difficult and time consuming.

What to Computerize

The first rule of thumb in computerized management is this: *Just because a task can be computerized is no reason to do it.* A number of tasks can be done more simply by hand than by machine. How do library media specialists judge whether a task should be computerized? The answer is probably a combination of experimentation and sharing experiences with colleagues before major decisions are made.

The major question is, "What type of library media operations can be profitably computerized?" The answer is to look for operations which are repetitive and require data manipulation or analysis. There are many repetitive operations which computers won't handle at this time, and shelving books is one example (although robotics may take care of this sooner than we imagine). Operations which have been successfully computerized include

Circulation:
Registration
Circulation of materials (partially and fully computerized)
Circulation of equipment
Overdues
Circulation analysis and reporting
Scheduling of equipment, materials, and facilities

Technical Services:
Fully computerized catalogs (completely replacing card catalogs)
Computerized catalogs of partial collections (such as paperback collections, audiovisual collections; single-medium collections, such as the record or filmstrip collection)
Authority lists (such as subject headings or authors' names)
Catalog card production and label preparation
Interconnection to other libraries through computer networks such as OCLC
In-depth indexing of materials (indexes to poetry and play collections)
Periodical check-in
Consideration files
Ordering

Reference Operations:
Bibliography generation
Files of reference questions and their answers
Community resource files
Locally created databases
Online database searching

Administration:
Collection analysis
Plans for units of instruction
Reports
Data analysis (circulation, borrowers, collection size)

Planning documents
Word processing
Notes to teachers

Perhaps the key is imagination. It takes a bit of creativity to decide a new way to save time and energy by using a microcomputer. It also takes many hours of experimentation and effort to get a method to function on a microcomputer and be reliable enough to be useful. When the task is complete, the computerized method should meet the following criteria:

1. The computerized method should save time. This means that it does the job in less time than a comparable task done by hand or by another machine.
2. The computerized method should be more accurate. When a human does a repetitive task, we make allowances for error. When the computer (and the human operating it) performs a task, the error rate should be at least as low (or lower) than the manual operation.
3. The computerized method should be more efficient. Do not think only of saving time but also of doing more work in the same amount of time. Oftentimes a task can be done by microcomputer that cannot be done manually because the manual task is much too much work. For example, the school library media specialist may be able to take inventory several times a year using a microcomputer and a light pen, where the same task is done annually (if that often) when individuals must do the task.
4. The computerized method must be easy. Sometimes, it will be so complicated that untrained workers or clerical personnel cannot do it. This returns the responsibility for the activity to the professional library media specialist and defeats the purpose of the original design.
5. The computerized method must be adaptable. School library media specialists must be able to integrate the method into ongoing administrative operations. If primary consideration must be given to the microcomputer in terms of where a task must be done, when it can be done, and precisely what must be done, then the microcomputer uses more time—time needed to plan how to meet its specifications rather than meeting management needs. If school library media specialists find that their days are planned around the microcomputer and what it can do, it is time to reconsider. Microcomputers are tools, not masters.
6. The computerized method must be cost effective. The microcomputer must do as much (or more) work for less money than a manual system. At times, it will be necessary to compute the time of professionals and clericals when costing out computerized methods vs. manual methods. Microcomputer hardware is just one cost to take into account. There are also

supplies, maintenance, and software costs to be totaled when thinking of using the microcomputer for management statistics.

A number of commercial products are already on the market which are designed to computerize an operation or can be used to design a local application. These products are generally of two types: targeted software or generic software.

Targeted and Generic Software

Targeted software is a package which was created to do a specific task, such as creating a bibliography or circulating materials. Generic software, on the other hand, is like the frame of a house. It provides a structure; the program user provides the furnishings and contents. An example of generic software is a word processor. The word processing package, which provides the structure, can be used to write letters, create bibliographies, edit lists, and so on. The author of the generic package is not sure how the user will use the software.

In addition, software can have one function or integrated functions. One-function software has been designed to do one thing well, and only one thing. Its single use may be to create bibliographies and nothing else. Integrated software uses a number of applications simultaneously. Thus, the data from one segment of the program will work in another segment. Table 1 categorizes the software available for computerizing library media operations. These categories should be examined more fully so that, as commercial packages are encountered by library media specialists, they can be categorized and judged a little more effectively.

One-Function Home-grown Software

Many brilliant beginning programmers, who attend schools today, are anxious to try out their newly learned skills. They can be enlisted to help create programs which will be useful to their school and to the library media center. However, expectations for high-quality work must be tempered with reality. If a simple product is required, a student may be able to create something that will work very well. On the other hand, a complex task will usually require an advanced programmer.

The advantage of home-grown products is that they are usually designed to do a task the way the library media specialist wants it done. If it works and does the job, the specialist is happy. The program may be unsophisticated and rigid, but no one is particularly concerned. Usually there is no better product on the market, or something is created that may fill a void in the commercial market.

Most good programs start with ideas from a practitioner who teams up with a programmer to create a program. The problem with sharing this type of program with another library media specialist is that it might not fit another situation. Using

TABLE 1.

Classification of Computer Software for Library Media Operations

Targeted Software

One-Function	*Integrated*
A. Software with Limited Usefulness a) Home-grown (created by the staff or purchased from others who created it for their own use) b) Commercial programs designed to do one thing easily and quickly Example: Bibliography Writer	A. N/A
B. Middle-Size Programs There is some flexibility, but the program usually has definite requirements which may or may not fit into the usual procedures Example: Winnebago Circulation System	B. Middle-Size Programs The data from one segment of the program will work in another segment. For example, a list of patron names is typed in only once and is used by both the circulation and the overdue programs
C. Large Systems These programs allow more flexibility but are isolated from other systems; i.e., data is not transferable to other programs. For example, the author and title information in an automated card catalog could not be used in a circulation program without being re-entered	C. Large Systems Flexibility is allowed, in addition to multiple use of data by various programs

Generic Software

Narrow Function	*Broad Function*
Created with a narrow range of uses in mind, even though it appears broad at first glance. Examples: PFS File, PFS Report, DB Master, D Base II, and AppleWorks	Complex and powerful. The creators are not sure of the range of uses. Example: Symphony I, Framework II

home-grown products means testing for success at the next location. A rule of thumb might be: Does the program work? Does it do what needs to be done? Does it do the job the way it should be done? If the answer to all questions is yes, use the locally developed program in the new location until something better comes along.

Where can one find these types of program? They are often donated by colleagues or can be secured from persons who attend computer user meetings; or they may be found in magazines where programs are listed, to be typed into the library media center's computer. They are also available in small ads in the back of library periodicals (beginning entrepreneurs can seldom afford large advertisements). While these programs are usually inexpensive, they are not always acceptable. One must try before buying, or at least verify that the product can be returned if it does not meet specifications or needs.

One-Function Commercial Programs

A number of commercial ventures have resulted from experiments by library media specialists who realize that there may be commercial gain in their computerized creations. Such an example was the Library Software Company and its product, Bibliography Writer. This program does one thing and does it well. It is so "user friendly" that it can be given to students with very little instruction. The advantage of this program is that items may be sorted a number of different ways, which makes it more useful than a word processor for the same task.

Commercial programs which perform one function are likely to be demonstrated at conferences and written up and reviewed in library media periodicals. They should do the jobs they were designed to do with a minimum number of problems. The cost should be reasonable and a good backup policy should be in effect.

Middle-Size Programs

A middle-size one-function program will usually work on a microcomputer which has one or two disk drives and 64 to 128K of memory. The Winnebago Circulation Program is such a program. It requires two disk drives, 64K, and a light pen; a printer is needed to print bar-code labels on the materials. A version for hard disk is also available. This program does only circulation; it is not a card catalog. To use it, the entire collection must be entered: both author and title, plus copy number of each if duplicates are held. These files, once created, cannot be used by another program for another purpose. This should not be taken as critical of this product, or any other product in this category. The creators have merely concentrated on doing one thing and doing it well. That is the criterion which must be used for judging.

Middle-size products often require a greater investment for both hardware and software. Usually one microcomputer must be dedicated to that specific use, and the software must be matched to the correct machine. For example, the microcomputer may have to be stationed at the circulation desk all day and be used *only* for circulation.

Selection of this type of management function requires careful planning. Has it been used in a location which can be visited? Will the vendor demonstrate and allow hands-on testing for one day? Will it really do the job you want and in the most efficient way? Are funds available to purchase both hardware and software and dedicate them to a single purpose?

Middle-size products may require specialized peripheral equipment to supplement the storage capacity of the microcomputer. Most often, a hard disk must be purchased to increase the computer's storage. School library media specialists must do much reading, talking, comparing, and planning before selecting one-function programs.

Integrated Middle-Size Programs

A number of middle-size programs are designed so that data from one segment of the program will work in another segment. The multifunction database is *integrated,* in computer software terminology. Computer Cat is an example of this type of program. In its latest edition (distributed by Winnebago), Computer Cat is not only an online catalog but will also serve as a circulation system, complete with overdues. This program requires a dedicated microcomputer with a hard-disk drive and is best installed where several terminals are linked together so that multiple users can search the database simultaneously. The advantage to these programs is that the entire collection is entered only once. That database is then used by the catalog program, the circulation program, and the overdue program.

Care will be needed to select both the software and hardware since the costs will be much higher, the time to get them going will be considerable, and "political" considerations begin to grow because of the great public relations factor inherent in such a decision. A visit to a location where this product is in use is essential before purchase. How do manufacturers' claims match the installed version? What happens when something goes wrong? How can such a large database be protected from being destroyed? Can the system be handled by the current staff, or will it be necessary to have a specialist on the staff to operate the program?

Large Systems with One or More Integrated Functions

A number of large systems on the market, such as CLSI and DATAPHASE, are targeted for very large school library media centers and public and academic libraries. These systems are expensive, require specially trained staff to operate them, and represent a major investment of money, time, and commitment. Their political consequences are considerable. If the system does not live up to expectations, it will become a white elephant. Major investments of time and planning are required before these systems are even considered for a school.

Generic Software with a Narrow Function

A number of programs, created for business applications, are also useful in the library media center (these programs are discussed in detail later). Generic software is valuable when the library media specialist takes the time to learn how to use it. For example, the documentation for "PFS File," an electronic filing cabinet, is very easy to understand and will take only three or four hours of work to create a useful product, such as a bibliography program or a community resource file. Other programs, such as DB Master and ProFILE III PLUS, will require considerable study time and experimentation before a useful product will emerge.

Many pre-created applications, called *templates,* are beginning to appear which make the use of these generic packages very simple. These templates are very valuable—to get, share, use, and modify. They will become commonplace in the literature as time passes.

Generic Software with a Broad Function

A number of very powerful programs that are beginning to appear on the market have multiple functions. They usually run on CP/M-based microcomputers that have 128K or more memory. Many of them have been created for the IBM PC or equivalent equipment, and Symphony I is an example. This multifunction program has a database manager, a spreadsheet program, a word processor, a communications package, and a graphic function all in one. The database manager will act as an automated filing cabinet, the spreadsheet as an automated ledger sheet, and the graphic package will help chart the data. When all of these files are combined with the powerful word processor included in the package, entire reports, complete with data, graphical analysis, and projections, can be created. These packages do not require as large an investment as one would think, but they do require a considerable investment of time to learn how to operate them if all their potential is to be realized.

To learn these packages, it is best to attend a short course or belong to a computer club that covers the topic regularly—or impose on a friend who uses them. The most frequent and efficient users of these packages are likely to come from the business world, and they may not know library media applications.

In all these applications, a few guidelines are in order:

1. Know exactly what data is to be filed and how it should be managed.
2. Know what the multifunction package will provide.
3. Understand what hardware is necessary to run the software.
4. Look carefully at the quality of documentation to the program.
5. Know who will help if problems arise.
6. Assess the cost to keep the program running after the initial investment.
7. When improvements are made in the program, the new edition should be available at reduced prices. *Note:* Beware the new edition that requires major changes in format of data or analysis. It may mean reentry of data or a different form of output.

When Programs Fail

Murphy's law applies to computerization of library management, as it does to most things. If something *can* go wrong, it *will*, and high hopes can be destroyed. Political pressure to automate can be intense, especially if the administration sees it as a labor-saving program pointing toward staff reduction. Sales pressure from vendors can be enormous, and the desire to be "in the forefront" can seem irresistible. What happens when the system fails to deliver what it was supposed to deliver, or just plain fails?

The more complex the system, the more chances for failure. Data can be lost, the electrical power can fail, the creator and seller of the program can move away or go out of business. What then?

Contingency plans are a must, but they too may fail. What then?

Sometimes one must admit failure. This does not mean that anyone is admitting defeat. Consider the experience a learning experiment. If the system does not work, stop. Attempting to repair it may increase its failure, or be more costly than should be or can be afforded. Do the task another way. Perhaps the old way wasn't so bad after all.

Of course, risks are taken. Management is filled with risks. If no one experiments with management applications on microcomputers, all library media specialists will be the losers. What would be tragic is not that one has tried and failed, but that school library media specialists do not try at all. Everyone must experiment and report those experiments to others. Reports of failures will be as important as the successes.

Many school library media specialists will wish to develop their own applications. The section which follows describes methods for creating school library media management software.

Creating Management Software

Richard E. Chase and Jane Klasing

When the first spreadsheets, database managers, and word processing programs for microcomputers were created in the early 1980s, the creators had business managers in mind. But in just a few years' time, these tools have become necessities for anyone who writes, manages, or deals with information—including every library media specialist. To say that library media specialists should be as comfortable with spreadsheets, database managers, and word processors as with the pencil does not overstate the case. Library media specialists already have a great deal of experience developing in-house procedures for handling circulation, book work, and budgeting. They often spend much time designing work flow, streamlining tasks, and redesigning operations. This same resourcefulness, combined with computer technology, provides a whole new arena for efficiency.

Many operational procedures in the library media center are candidates for automation, but there is enough difference in the techniques used that it is unlikely that commercial programs will ever be developed to handle all techniques. Consequently, most managers need tools to assist them in the development of ways to handle specific tasks tailored to individual needs.

There are two ways to create software to deal with library media management operations. The first is to make use of the generic programs of word processing, database managers, and spreadsheets. The second is to create programs from scratch which will handle specific tasks. In case the reader is unfamiliar with these programs, a word processor can be thought of as an automated typewriter, a database manager as an automated filing cabinet, and a spreadsheet as a computerized general ledger. Generally, the first time one learns a word processor-database manager-spreadsheet program, there is a fair amount of mental exertion and anguish, but persistence usually produces genuine satisfaction.

Generic Management Programs

There are many generic management programs on the market for a variety of computers. Brand names of these programs are familiar because of advertising, e.g., AppleWorks, PFS File/Report/Write, Symphony, Lotus 1-2-3, Enable are just a few.

In just five years, there has been such an improvement in the capabilities of these management programs that those who learned a commercial program early are likely to find themselves at a disadvantage. However, after the rudiments are learned, moving on to more sophisticated programs and techniques is not difficult and is worth the effort.

The advantage of the generic programs over commercial programs is generally price. Hundreds of management tasks can be done with generic programs at a fraction of the cost of commercial programs designed to do only one function well. Another advantage is that whatever the application, the operation of the generic program is basically the same. Every commercial program is different in the way it runs, the commands needed to run it, and a multitude of other idiosyncrasies.

The best advice, in absence of a crystal ball, is to choose the most sophisticated integrated package that will run on the available hardware. In an integrated package, word processing, database management and spreadsheet capabilities are all in a single program and are present simultaneously in the computer so that the operator can switch back and forth almost instantly. The commands used in one part of the program are very similar to the commands used in another section. Integrated programs generally require a large random access memory (RAM) in the computer, and so often hardware must be modified. For example, Apple-Works requires a 128K minimum to operate efficiently. Nevertheless, if very large files are anticipated, it would be wise to increase the memory to half a megabyte and beyond, e.g., programs such as Symphony require over 300K to operate.

There are also a number of commercial programs available which have limited integration. This means that word processing-database manager-spreadsheet capabilities will be three separate programs, but the information stored on disks can be used in any of the three programs when they are run. Examples are PFS File, PFS Report, PFS Write, PFS Graph, PFS Access. Many library media specialists have found this series so easy to use that they do not mind having to leave one program and start another to be able to combine word processed letters from PFS Write with database information created on PFS File.

A third choice is to select three different products which do their functions very well but are not compatible. For example, one might choose for word processing, Apple Writer; for a database manager, DB Master; and for a spreadsheet, Super-Calc. Each of these programs does things that a totally integrated package may not be able to do, but their information cannot be shared and there are three totally separate programs to learn.

Many library media specialists have learned programs that were easily available in the school and that matched the available hardware—Bank Street Writer, for example. While these types of programs are good for an introduction to management applications, they are not likely to be sophisticated enough to accomplish the tasks which need to be done in the library media center.

Some library media specialists may wish to start with simpler programs and grow into larger and more sophisticated ones. Others may just start with the sophisticated package. The approach depends on the programs and help available, as well as on courage and dogged persistence. Either way, the effort expended is worth the struggle.

Using Database Management Programs

With a database management system, one can store information on a disk and then print it out in a number of different ways. The commercial program comes as a skeleton and the user creates the plan for what information will be entered, how it will be entered, how it will be sorted, and how it will be printed out. Known as a template, the plan prepares the database management program to receive the information needed and provides a way to manipulate that information in a variety of useful ways.

The names of many of the available database management systems are familiar: DB Master, dBASE II, Quick File, PFS File (Report and Graph), Lotus 1-2-3, Symphony, and Jazz. However, these programs have certain equipment requirements which will have to be dealt with before the program is purchased. Most programs require a minimum of 128K to operate.

The advantage of a generic database program is that many different databases can be created and each may be tailored to local needs; each application created will be used basically the same way. The program therefore will be less expensive to buy than a number of single-application packages.

The major problem with database management systems is that they take substantial time and effort to learn—at least 20 hours of intense study and experimentation. After studying the problem, one of the authors decided to create the templates at the district level, where the expertise was available, and then the building-level library media specialists could use the templates very easily and, with minimum time and effort, learn the system. Also, a number of templates are published in library literature which can considerably shorten the time it takes to learn a database system.

A database manager which is likely to serve the needs of the library media center should meet a number of general selection criteria. The following criteria might be useful in choosing among competing systems.

1. The support materials are effective and comprehensive.
2. The user can design screens for data entry.
3. The program can be exited easily, and from any mode.
4. The program is reliable in normal use.
5. The logistics in handling the program are manageable.
6. The user can change or add to the fields established for data entry.
7. Data and utility disks are separate from the program disks.
8. Replacement and backup copies are available.
9. Commands and prompts are consistent throughout.
10. The program provides both a delete and edit mode.
11. The program allows bypass of particular fields during data entry.
12. Search by specified range, partial match, or by using multiple fields is permitted.
13. Search time is acceptable.
14. Sort and merge time is acceptable.
15. The user is allowed to customize the system to the printer.

Once the database management package is selected, an intense study and experimentation period should begin. Figure 1, showing two sample templates created for DB Master, should give an idea of how a sample file might be set up.

FIGURE 1. An Equipment Inventory Template

Fields Set Up on Screen	Sample Entry in the Fields
CODE	CODE—MICRO 01
BPI #	BPI #—8217091
SERIAL #	SERIAL #—319578
MANUFACTURER	MANUFACTURER—30
MODEL	MODEL—APPLE II
LAMP	LAMP—_____
DATE/PURCHASE	DATE/PURCHASE—02/25/82
COST	COST—$1454.00
LOCATION	LOCATION—MEDIA CENTER 01
COMMENTS	COMMENTS—SECURITY REPORT 9/8/83
COMMENTS	COMMENTS—_____

An Equipment Inventory Template

The fields (categories of information) created for the system are shown in figure 1.

When the data are all entered, a sample printout with just some of the categories entered but in order of the code would look as shown in figure 2. Items on the printout can be arranged in any order or style including or excluding any item in the original database. The data format statements required by DB Master to create the above report would look as shown in figure 3. The sort requirements, allowing the program to sort on any field and printout the report in that order, would look like figure 4.

FIGURE 2. Sample Printout

01-25-85			INVENTORY/CODE		PAGE 1
CODE	SERIAL #	BPI #	MANUFAC.	LOCATION	MODEL
CR01	00006409	7415185	420	PROF. LIB.	2551
CR02	25208999	8121260	420	PROF. LIB.	2502
MICRO 01	8217091	319578	30	MEDIA CENTER 01	APPLE II

FIGURE 3. Format Statements

```
DATA FMAT — INVENTORY/AV
REPORT WIDTH = 79
COLUMN TITLE LINES:
          CODE              SERIAL #       BPI #           MANUFACTURER
. . . DATA LINE #1 . . .
FIELD #1: CODE             TAB = 2        LENGTH = 12
FIELD #2: SERIAL #         TAB = 6        LENGTH = 22
FIELD #3: BPI #            TAB = 6        LENGTH = 15
FIELD #4: MANUFACTURER     TAB = 11       LENGTH = 3
FIELD #5: LOCATION         TAB = 20       LENGTH = 15
FIELD #6: MODEL            TAB = 32       LENGTH = 12
```

FIGURE 4. Sort Requirements

```
ST FORMAT — INVENTORY/CODE
SORT #            FIELD NAME
   1              CODE

SELECT FMAT = ALL RECORDS
FIELD NAME          OPERATION & TEST VALUE
* * * * *    ALL RECORDS      * * * * *
```

Bibliography Template

Another useful application for the database manager is the bibliography template, which will allow the construction of subject bibliographies that can be revised frequently. The fields can be designed to include books, audiovisual materials, and periodical articles. The database management system will permit the development of bibliographies with large numbers of entries. The entries can then be sorted and printed out in any order desired. One such format is shown in figure 5.

While only two sample applications have been given here, many other applications could be built and used. A few ideas are:

1. Collect management statistics of many types and print out reports (some programs such as PFS File, PFS Report, and PFS Graph allow you to chart the statistics).
2. Keep a file of difficult-to-answer reference questions categorized under numerous subject headings.

FIGURE 5. Bibliography Template

Fields Set Up on the Screen

```
TITLE
CT.
CONT.
AUTHOR
PUB/PRODUCER
DATE
PAGES
TYPE/MATERIAL
CALL #
```

Type of material key:
1 Books
2 Audiovisual materials
3 Periodical articles

Sample Entry in the Fields

```
TITLE—Teaching Computer Literacy: Gu
CT.—idelines for a Six-Week Course
CONT.—for Teachers
AUTHOR—Anderson, Cheryl
PUB/PRODUCER—Electronic Learning
DATE—November 1981,
PAGES—pp. 30–31.
TYPE/MATERIAL—3
CALL #—_____

TITLE—How to Operate the Apple II + a
CONT.—nd the Apple IIe
CONT.—_____
AUTHOR—_____
PUB/PRODUCER—SVE
DATE—_____
PAGES—_____
TYPE/MATERIAL—2
CALL #—CD 001.64

TITLE—Staff Development, Part II.
CT.—_____
CONT.—_____
AUTHOR—Griffin, Gary A.
PUBL/PRODUCER—Chicago: U. of Chicago,
DATE—1983.
PAGES—_____
TYPE/MATERIAL—1
CALL #—370.7 GR
```

3. Record any necessary lists.
4. Create a catalog for a paperback book collection (under 2,000 titles).
5. Build a catalog of special collections, such as art prints or computer software.
6. Construct a patron identification list.
7. Establish a catalog and circulation system for a reserve collection.
8. Formulate a periodical check-in system and claim printout.
9. Index a collection of poetry or plays.

All the above and more can be accomplished on a regular 64K microcomputer with two disk drives. Projects that require larger amounts of data will require a hard disk with storage capacity in the millions of bytes.

Another source of assistance for database templates is Eric S. Anderson's newsletter entitled *The Wired Librarian*. With the support of the Highsmith Company, Anderson offers a national clearinghouse for library management applications and application templates. Library media specialists who have an application format using Apple versions of VisiCalc, DB Master, and AppleWorks and are willing to share should contact the Highsmith Company for details. In this way library media specialists can become users by benefiting from the successful experiences of others who have systems in operation.

Using Word Processing Programs

Word processing is truly a twentieth-century innovation. What the typewriter did for handwritten documents, word processing is doing for typewritten documents. There is little need for a typewriter in the library media center except for a few mundane quick chores such as typing a book card or addressing an envelope. All other writing is done better and faster using a word processing program. With a single typing, word processing programs have the unique capability of moving, inserting, and deleting text; providing underlining and super and subscripts; and formatting documents. Manuscripts are easily revised without retyping the entire manuscript. Thus, any writing done in the library media center can benefit from a word processing program.

Popular word processing programs include AppleWorks, Apple Writer, Volkswriter, Perfect Writer, and a score of others. There are also a number of nonsophisticated programs such as Bank Street Writer, the Milliken Word Processor, Magic Slate, and others. Generally, it is a good idea to choose a word processing program that is sophisticated enough to do a detailed college research paper. Choosing a more sophisticated package ensures enough features to handle just about any task that comes along. The library media specialist is likely to grow out of a student-oriented package rather quickly. If a word processing program is included in an integrated program such as AppleWorks, then the library media specialist will be likely to have the power and sophistication needed. If a program must be selected which is not compatible with the database program or spreadsheet being used, then try to select one that is as similar as possible. A program such as Wordstar 2000 may be too sophisticated for the average library media specialist, but even the Cadillacs of the business can handle the mundane and the operator can always grow into the sophisticated program as projects demand.

It is particularly good to choose a word processing program which colleagues are using so that disks, formats, and data files can be shared through a disk-swapping arrangement or over telephone lines. The newer word processing programs provide ways to convert files from one microcomputer to another. For example, this chapter was first typed into Apple Writer then transferred to AppleWorks for final editing. More and more publishers and organizations are accepting reports, articles, and news features on disk rather than on paper but compatible word processing programs are required for sharing.

What can a word processing program be used for in library media centers? Letters for free materials (change only the name and address each time), notes to faculty, notes to students, lists, reports, bibliographies; in short, anything written. Word processing saves a great deal of time when repetitive writing is demanded with only minor changes. A memorandum to faculty, for example, can contain several general paragraphs and several directed to specific faculty members or departments. The general paragraphs need not be retyped. Annual reports can be updated easily by changing the dates and a few figures and leaving other information intact.

If the library media specialist is already familiar with a word processing package and thinks a more sophisticated package is needed, the best advice is to try the new package. The transition is not too difficult; soon the old package will seem outmoded and useless (that is, if the new program actually is better). Occasionally, it may be wise to keep the first word processing programs because of special features. For example, Apple Writer (ProDos version) can handle wide charts but AppleWorks can't.

Word processing programs require printers. Dot matrix printers are much faster than letter-quality printers but their print quality is not as good. As a general rule, the better the image quality and the faster the speed, the more the printer will cost. A good dot matrix printer can often suffice for the production of catalog cards and general correspondence. If letter quality is required, both types of printers should be purchased. The dot matrix printer will be used when speed is required; the letter quality when fine copy is needed.

Be sure that the word processing programs purchased will support the printer purchased. Can the printer underline? set super and subscript? print in pica, elite, and compressed print? The word processing program should be able to communicate to the printer the commands needed to do these special tasks. Many hours can be spent trying to give the correct signals in the program so that the printer will underline. It is always good to check the documentation on the word processing program to see which printers the program will support. Many printers will work with almost any microcomputer, but learning how to make them compatible can be very frustrating. This chapter was printed on a Qume Letter Pro 20 printer hooked to an Apple computer and utilizing AppleWorks. It took a full two days work to get AppleWorks to communicate properly with the printer. AppleWorks was created to communicate with Apple printers and then with others by special commands. Once the two machines know how to communicate with one another everything is fine. In this case, machines are not unlike human beings.

Using Spreadsheets as Management Programs

Spreadsheets are automated ledgers. They are made up of rows and columns to which the user assigns fixed headings. The rows and columns intersect in cells. The honeycombed cells, illustrated in figure 6, receive the variable data—words or numbers. Within cells formulas may be inserted for adapting the data to the purpose of the spreadsheet.

Because cells can be lengthened, as illustrated in figure 7, cells can contain phrases or sentences. Since the spreadsheet can be arranged, using words in the cells can turn the spreadsheet into a database that has some advantages true databases do not.

VisiCalc was the first microcomputer spreadsheet, and it became an immensely popular program with business persons. It is no longer marketed, but its descendants such as SuperCalc, AppleWorks, Multiplan, Lotus 1-2-3, and PC-Calc are readily available. Spreadsheets come in varying sizes, usually based on the amount of memory available and the limits of the program. Many can have over 200 rows and 125 columns; others can have thousands of rows and columns. For a school library media center, the smaller spreadsheet size will do many things.

FIGURE 6. Spreadsheet Cells

FIGURE 7. Lengthened Spreadsheet Cells

The most popular use of spreadsheets is to keep budgetary information, calculation, and budgetary forecasts. As with databases, a template must first be created and then the data entered. A simple budget spreadsheet, figure 8, is from May Lein Ho's *AppleWorks for School Librarians* published by Hi Willow Research and Publishing. The spreadsheet may not seem very impressive since the same budget is easily put on a single ledger sheet and the columns added with a calculator. However, columns could be added to the right which would detail the amounts spent from each encumberance on parts of the collection. For example, columns could be made for general collection, folklore, animals, dinosaurs, frontier, Indians, space travel, junior novels, etc. Segments of the collection being built could be tracked very easily for reports to administrators detailing where funds have been spent. The advantage of the spreadsheet is that columns can be added, deleted, amounts changed, new totals calculated—all without having to re-enter numbers or columns already in the spreadsheet.

At budget time, several budget proposals are easily constructed using proposed or actual funds in various categories such as local, state, federal, and gift funds. Funds needed to increase the collection size by a percentage each year can be calculated easily.

Besides budgets, spreadsheets can be used for keeping inventory figures, calculation and control of fines, analysis of questionnaire data, calculation of grades, analysis of any library media statistics, collection analysis by age or circulation per user, orders for supplies with columns totaled, book or AV material orders with prices totaled, etc. In short, any process which requires calculation of any kind can be stored in the spreadsheet and manipulated very easily.

FIGURE 8.   Budget Spreadsheet

File: Budget 1
Page 1

Jan. 1986

Month	To Spend	Paid: To Whom	Books	AV	Mags.	Supplies	Software	Total
Jan	$1,000.00							$1,000.00
Jan		369 Supply				$36.00		
Jan		B. Dalton	$36.25					
Jan		EBSCO			$190.00			
Jan		Highsmith				$200.00		
Jan		Scholastic		$300.00				
Tot. Exp.			$36.25	$300.00	$190.00	$236.00		$762.25
Percent			3.62%	30.00%	19.00%	23.60%		76.22%
Balance								$237.75

Programming Your Own Software

Often the school library media specialist wishes to computerize a specialized library media task. In this case, it may seem best to create the program locally. This decision takes courage, confidence, and time commitment. However, the reason for undertaking such a task is simple—the best ideas for management applications in the library media center come from people working in the center, not from programmers who have never worked in a center.

If school library media specialists truly wish to program their own software, there are some programming skills which are prerequisite to beginning. One should know the rudiments of programming, such as screen formatting, IF—THEN, FOR—NEXT, and similar commands. In addition one will need to understand READ and DATA statements, sequential files, and random files. It is necessary to have sorting routines available also. It may be possible to learn these skills from many computer guides on the market or to take a course that covers files, sorts, and arrays at a university or a technical school.

Armed with programming skill (or a good student programmer or an adult volunteer who is willing to help), one can begin to build an idea and then program it. The school library media specialist must know exactly what should be done and the exact form of the product. For example, in creating an overdue notice, it must be decided what information is necessary for each overdue item.

1. What is the minimum amount of information necessary?
2. What additional information might be nice to have?

The problem one encounters is that the more information that is needed, the more elaborate the program and the more space each item will take on the disk. The more space on the disk each item takes, the fewer items can be stored. For example, it may be decided that the minimum information is the book title, patron name, and patron address (a room number). In addition, the call number, the date due, and the homeroom teacher's name would be helpful.

Next it must be decided exactly how the computer is to print the overdue records. All or some of the following may be necessary:

1. An overdue notice for each patron (addressed and ready to send out) which lists all items overdue. This notice should contain some standard message such as ''The above materials are overdue and must be returned or renewed today.''
2. A list of all the overdue books arranged by patron's last name.
3. A list of all the overdue books arranged by title and/or author.
4. A list of all the overdue books arranged by homeroom and subarranged by patron name.
5. A procedure for deleting returned items and sending out second and third notices plus a final bill.

The examples shown in figures 9 and 10 are taken from an overdue notice program created by one of the authors for his high school in Red Wing, Minnesota. In addition to the printouts shown, there is a printout arranged by item number. Each overdue item is given an accession number and then is deleted by that number from the computer. The program has been designed so that it is easy to enter items that are overdue, delete them, and print out overdue notices or lists. The program is simple enough to be handled by student assistants and/or clerical workers. An overdue list is kept at the checkout desk. If an item is returned, it is crossed off the list when the item is carded and deleted from the computer once a week when overdue notices are printed.

The above program was developed before any commercial programs to handle overdues became available on the commercial market. Now that there are several overdue programs available, the library media specialist must take a second look at a homemade system. How does it compare with the commercial product? Which program is more useful? Which is easier? Which does the job better? The answers to these questions may not always favor the commercial product.

FIGURE 9.   Overdue Notice

OVERDUE NOTICE

ALBRECHT BECKY	PERIOD 1	ROOM 211
COMPLETE NOVELS C1	CRA	DUE 12/19/83
SPOON RIVER C1	821.008MAS	DUE 12/19/83

THE ABOVE MATERIALS ARE OVERDUE AND MUST BE RETURNED OR RENEWED TODAY

FIGURE 10.   The Overdue Book List by Student Name

OVERDUE BOOK LIST—PAGE 1

NAME	BOOK DESCRIPTION	CALL #	DATE DUE	RM	PER
ALBRECHT BECKY	SPOON RIVER C1	821.0008MAS	12/19/83	211	1
ALBRECHT BETH	FAMILY HEALTH	FAM070080	02/06/84	103	1
ANDERSON DUANE	BASIC TELEVISION C1	621.388ZBA	12/19/83	104	2
ANDERSON RODNEY	STAND C1	KING	01/15/84	154	3
BORN CONNIE	ASK FOR LOVE	ANG	02/03/84	116	2
BURT JENNY	SHINING C1	KING	01/15/84	211	1
CONNIFF DIANE	EBONY	EBO120079	01/15/84	103	2
DURAY DORIS	TAPE RECORDER	TAPAV211	02/06/84	125	3
HOLMQUIST J	ALL THE PRESI C.1	BERN	12/19/83	104	3

Control and Service

Creating management software by using generic word processing programs, database managers and spreadsheets, and, on occasion, programming some software is a new concept for school library media specialists. Those who venture into this area and overcome initial anxieties and frustrations generally gain not only a sense of satisfaction but also a new sense of power over their programs. The tools described in this chapter provide a new perspective—an analytic perspective on library media program and operations. Used properly, these tools can help the manager step back with a cold and logical precision to examine what is really going on in a library media center. In addition, so many new sources of informational databases can be constructed to serve the patron in ways that card catalogs and published indexes never could. Finally, communication with patrons, administrators, and parents is improved, and all this happens without an increased investment in time or effort.

Cataloging
Microcomputer Software

Nancy B. Olson

Traditionally, school library media specialists have done their own cataloging or purchased catalog cards from book dealers or jobbers. In contrast, public and academic librarians have purchased cards from the Library of Congress ever since those cards became available in 1901. Librarians in large public libraries and academic libraries have participated in the development of bibliographic utilities such as OCLC (Online Computer Library Center, Inc.) in an effort to reduce duplication in cataloging and to develop shared databases which facilitate interlibrary loan of materials and other activities.

The ideal in shared cataloging would be to have an item cataloged by one cataloger. Catalogers in all other libraries could use that bibliographic record, rather than duplicate the effort and cost. In this utopian situation, all librarians would agree to use the same cataloging rules in order to create bibliographic records that would be uniform throughout the network.

The cataloging rules accepted as standard in this country are the *Anglo-American Cataloguing Rules,* second edition (*AACR2*), published in 1978 by the American Library Association, the Canadian Library Association, and the Library Association (of Great Britain). In addition to these rules, which cover description only, almost all school library media specialists rely on the latest editions of the *Abridged Dewey Decimal Classification System* and *Sears Subject Headings.*

The basic idea underlying *AACR2* is that the first part of the bibliographic description (title through statement of responsibility) shows *exactly* the information given on the chief source of information (usually the title page or its substitute). The rest of the bibliographic description gives any other important information from the title page, back of the title page (verso), book jacket, other front pages, or their equivalents in nonbook materials. When librarians share their cataloging and

83

use the same set of rules, everyone is assured of uniformity and more consistent catalogs and indexes.

Cataloging of any nonbook material has always been a challenge; only with the development of *AACR2* were all types of materials included in one set of rules. Since the international rules did not deal with nonbook materials very well before *AACR2*, numerous organizations and state departments of education gave assistance to school library media specialists by publishing cataloging manuals. This proliferation of manuals has encouraged divergence of practice. Since 1978, the trend has been to accept the international standard and national databases (such as OCLC) to coordinate all efforts.

While *AACR2* includes rules for describing computer programs in its chapter 9, entitled "Machine-Readable Data Files," this chapter was written before the advent of microcomputer software. Thus, the chapter lacks much needed for dealing with this type of media. To compensate, the Resources and Technical Services Division of the American Library Association published a pamphlet entitled *Guidelines for Using AACR2 Chapter 9 for Cataloging Microcomputer Software* in 1984. This publication was not intended to replace *AACR2* chapter 9 but to supplement it. National and international committees are still working toward an internationally acceptable standard.

It would seem that the rules could be revised quickly to deal with each new technology, but revision is not that easy. *AACR2* can only be changed through a process involving a joint committee made up of representatives from four countries: Great Britain, Canada, Australia, and the United States. Each country has its own special committees, all with their own ideas. The process of rule revision moves with agonizing slowness! At best, what can be presented here is the current thinking of the various ALA and international cataloging committees in the hope that the final revision will be close to that stated here. Library media specialists are advised to watch for the publication of a revised set of rules.

Terminology. One of the major problems with microcomputer software is that terminology changes so rapidly. A search of recent literature found the term *diskette* being replaced by the terms *disk* or *floppy disk.* The term *microcomputer* is being used, as are the terms *home computer, personal computer,* and *desktop computer.* The term *video game* is used for both the game systems, such as Odyssey and Intellivision, and the game software made for microcomputers, such as the Apple. With this in mind, the national committee has recommended use of the terms *disk* and *computer* rather than any variations which have been developing.

Rules for Describing Microcomputer Software

The rules and suggestions given here follow the recommendations of the *Guidelines,* rule interpretation by the Library of Congress, and a few personal interpretations. Parts of this section are taken from Nancy B. Olson, *A Manual of AACR2 Examples for Microcomputer Software and Video Games,* second edition (Lake Crystal, Minn.: Soldier Creek Press, 1985). When *AACR2* or *Guidelines* is cited here, it is paraphrased. Any personal interpretations are indicated. The rules cover microcomputer software and also electronic toys or games that are typically issued in cartridge carriers and manipulated by hand controls.

Chief Source of Information. The chief source of information when cataloging microcomputer software is the title screen(s) or title and credits screens. Some programs do not include title screens. When they do not or when libraries do not have access to microcomputers for cataloging, the information may be taken from the following sources (in order): disk label, container or package, or guide (manual, etc.). If such information is not available, the cataloger must supply a title, which will be bracketed.

Note: If a package contains other media, such as sound cassettes or videodiscs, in addition to the computer material, the package is considered to be a kit and is cataloged by *AACR2* rule 1.10.

Title and Statement of Responsibility Area. Use the same rules applied to books and other materials. Use the title that appears on the title screen(s) of the computer program. Transcribe it exactly except for punctuation and capitalization.

1. *General Material Designation (GMD).* Use of a GMD is optional. If it is used, it appears right after the main title, in square brackets, and before a subtitle or other title information. The current GMD for computer software is "machine-readable data file."
2. *Other Title Information.* Transcribe any other title information that appears on the title screen(s). Other title information not in the chief source of information may be put in a note.
3. *Statement of Responsibility.* Record statements of responsibility that appear prominently in the item in the form in which they appear. If a statement of responsibility is taken from a source other than the title screen(s), enclose it in square brackets. This means that the cataloger may include the names of anyone who had a major part in the creation and production of the software after determining if the person contributed enough to merit a listing on the catalog record.

Edition Area. This information may be taken from the title screen(s), the disk label, container, or guide. Several terms used on microcomputer software will indicate that the material has been published earlier in a different form. The terms *version, revision, edition,* or their abbreviations all indicate that the material previously existed in some different form and are to be used as edition statements. Usually the term will be followed by some kind of number, which is to be transcribed into the edition area along with the term. The term used is not to be abbreviated unless it is abbreviated on the item.

Examples: Vers. 2.1
Rev. 3-13-84

One must be careful to distinguish between a version of the operating system needed to run the computer software and the version of the software itself. The phrase "DOS version 3.3" refers to the version of the operating system. Indication of the operating system will usually include the letters "OS" or "CP/M."

Publication and Distribution Area. Follow the normal rules for this area. Record the place of publication and add the name of the country, state, and province, if necessary. Give the name of a publisher and/or distributor in the shortest form by which it can be understood and identified. Give the date of publication of the current version of the program you have in hand.

Physical Description Area. This area generates the greatest controversy among national and international committees. The best professional recommendations in the opinion of the author are:

Start with the physical entity:

1 computer disk (floppy or a hard disk)
1 computer cassette (looks like an audio cassette)
1 computer cartridge (a silicon chip and circuitry in a plastic container designed to plug into the microcomputer; often called a video game cartridge)

Add the brand name of the computer needed to run the software:

1 computer disk (Apple IIe)
1 computer cassette (Commodore 64)

One may add other physical details such as:

sound (if sound is heard, record "sd.")
color (if the display is in color, record "col.")
size
If the software is manufactured to fit only a specific machine, don't record the size. If it is not, use: size of computer disk ("5¼ in." or "8 in." or "3½ in.")
size of computer cassette (give only if nonstandard)
size of computer cartridge (give only if nonstandard)

Examples:

1 computer disk (Apple IIe) ; 5¼"
1 computer cassette (Commodore 64)
1 computer disk (Tandy 1000) : sd. col. ; 5¼"

Add accompanying material with the disks, cartridges, or cassettes. The number *1* is optional. When listing the items accompanying the software, use the name of the item as given on it when possible, e.g., teacher's guide, user's guide, or student manual.

> 1 computer disk (Apple IIe) ; 5¹/4″ + 1 teacher's guide.
> 1 computer cassette (Commodore 64) + 1 rule book + campaign strategy pad.
> 1 computer cartridge + cartridge instructions.
> 1 computer disk (TRS 80) + 1 teacher's manual + student manual (25 copies).

The container may be named if desired, and its size given if it would be helpful to a patron or if it causes unusual packing or shelving arrangements.

> 1 computer disk (Apple IIe) : 5¹/4″ + 1 teacher's guide, in box.
> 1 computer cartridge + cartridge instructions, in looseleaf binder.

Series Area. If an item is one of a series, record the title of the series. If the item belongs to two or more series, make separate series statements and enclose each statement in parentheses.

Notes Area. All notes are optional, but any or all may be included. If used, they must be in a certain order. Information from several types of notes may be combined into one. The three notes most useful to users of microcomputer software in schools are explained below. Catalogers may consult *AACR2* for details of the 22 specific notes allowed.

1. *System Requirements Note.* This note tells the user what is needed to use the item. The note begins with the words "System requirements:" and includes the make and model of microcomputer and any special requirements. The information is taken from anywhere on the title screen(s), disk label, container, or documentation. Frequently little or none of this information is given, in which case the note will be shortened or not added.

The first item named in the note is the make and model of microcomputer. This information is followed by a semicolon.

> System requirements: Apple II or higher;
> System requirements: IBM PC;

Add the amount of memory required. This information is followed by a semicolon. The author suggests that this information be included only if unusual.

> System requirements: Apple II or higher; 128K;
> System requirements: IBM-PC; 512K;

Add the operating system required to use the software.

System requirements: Apple II or higher; 128K; proDOS;
System requirements: IBM-PC; 512K; PCDOS 3.1;

Add any other special hardware requirements separated by commas. This information could include mention of more than one disk drive, a color monitor, printer, special printer, game paddles, joysticks, etc.

System requirements: Apple II or higher; 128K; proDOS; 2 disk drives, color monitor, printer.
System requirements: Apple IIe; 128K; proDOS; 4 disk drives, graphics printer.
System requirements: IBM-PC; 132 column printer.
System requirements: Commodore PET; joysticks.

2. *Summary Note.* This note tells the user about the item and what the item is used for. It should be brief and objective; it does not have to include complete sentences. It may not be needed if the title indicates clearly the purpose of the material or if a contents note makes the content of the package clear.

Summary: Word processing program.
Summary: Arithmetic games for use by individual students in grades 2–6.
Summary: Simulation game on wildlife management for use by groups of students in grades 6–12; takes about 20 min. to run.
Summary: Spelling tutorials for individual students in grades 2–8 with sixteen levels within each of three groups (grades 2–4, 5–6, 7–8). Eight lessons per level.

3. *Contents Note.* This note lists the contents of those packages containing several separately titled programs. The title of each program is listed, and a brief note about each may be included. Title added entries may be made for each title if desired.

Contents: ABC time — Spelling zoo — Letter game.
Contents: Legacy (multiplication game) — Alcohol (effects of alcohol) — Birthday (kaleidoscopic colored design) — Coin tossing (simulation of coin tosses with averages).

Access Points

Choosing the Main Entry. Use the same rules for choosing the main entry for microcomputer software as are applied to any other material. Try to determine the principal person responsible for the intellectual content of the software. Sometimes this will be a "creator," but it can be a programmer. If a creator merely hired a programmer to program an idea, the credit goes to the creator; the programmer, if important, could appear in an added entry. Corporate bodies will be used as the main entry only when the program is an official program of corporate thought, such as a catalog (on a microcomputer disk) of a professional collection in a school district. In most cases, a personal author or title main entry will be used for microcomputer courseware.

If corporate authorship is unknown, diffuse, or cannot be determined, enter under title.

Choosing Added Entries. As with other materials, make an added entry for each person, corporate body, and title under which a patron might look for information in the catalog. The company of production may be traced, but this information is of doubtful use in school library media centers. The microcomputer needed for the program may also be traced, although this would be of dubious value in school library media centers as well.

    I. Apple IIe.   II. Sunburst Communications.

Levels of Cataloging

A useful feature of *AACR2* is the three different levels of detail provided for bibliographic description. Level 1 is brief cataloging and is most appropriate for school library media centers. Levels 2 and 3 are for larger libraries and research institutions. School library media specialists should realize that they may use level 1 and add to it any details they feel their patrons need to know. As a reminder, figure 1 shows the minimum information in a level 1 description for a title main entry. An author main entry is shown in figure 2.

FIGURE 1.   Title Main Entry

Call no.	Title proper, — Edition statement. — First publisher, date of publication. Extent of item. Notes. Tracings.

FIGURE 2.   Author Main Entry

Call no.	Main Entry.
	    Title proper / first statement of responsibility if different from the main entry. — Edition statement. — First publisher, date of publication.
	    Extent of item.
	
	Notes.
	
	Tracings.

One of the cataloger's problems is a general materials designation, the identification of media type. If it is used, it belongs right after the title proper and before any subtitle. Library media specialists may prefer to use the GMD as a code in the call number. Another solution is to print the GMD in the upper left corner of the catalog card in lieu of a color band or a code, as shown in figures 3a and 3b. Words are much easier for the patron to understand than codes or colors.

FIGURE 3a. GMD designation in upper left corner of card

Machine readable data file

   978.3   Brown, Mike.
   B   On the Oregon Trail . . .

FIGURE 3b. Simplified GMD designation

Microcomputer software

   978.3   Brown, Mike.
   B   On the Oregon Trail . . .

Subject Headings

Use the same subject heading list for microcomputer software as for other materials. Adding headings not in *Sears* in the proper way standardizes the terms in the card catalog and makes subject searching much easier for the patron.

When choosing subject headings for microcomputer products, consider the subject of the program as well as its use.

OREGON TRAIL (use for a book about the Oregon Trail and for a simulation game)

For Operation Frog, microcomputer software showing how to dissect a frog, use the same subject heading as for a book about dissection of frogs: FROGS— ANATOMY.

A subdivision may be added to topical headings if desired:

OREGON TRAIL—COMPUTER ASSISTED INSTRUCTION

OREGON TRAIL—COMPUTER PROGRAM

For simulations, *Sears* gives the authority to add the names of types of games. Therefore, it is appropriate to use the following subject headings:

SIMULATION GAMES

SIMULATION GAMES IN EDUCATION (LC subject heading)

The following sample names of computer languages and computers may be used as models for subject headings:

BASIC (COMPUTER PROGRAMMING LANGUAGE)

IBM PERSONAL COMPUTER

APPLE IIe (COMPUTER)

Classification

Classifying all nonbook materials using the Dewey decimal system is the best idea. Even when materials are stored in cabinets away from the public, some organizational scheme is needed, and location by subject is easier than using accession numbers and always having to consult an index.

Using the abridged Dewey decimal system for computer software presents the same challenges as other nonbook media; i.e., *Dewey* was created as a book classification system, and sometimes numbers are assigned to nonbook media that don't make a great deal of sense.

Recognizing that computer science and computer hardware and software have changed drastically in the last few years, Forest Press, the publishers of *Dewey* have now issued a pamphlet entitled *004-006 Data Processing and Computer Science and Changes in Related Disciplines: Revision of Edition 19*, prepared by Julianne Beall in 1985. While this pamphlet does not revise the abridged *Dewey,* its suggestions will be incorporated into the next abridged edition.

Using the guidance of the new chapter, the following rules are given to help classify computer books and computer software.

1. Classify computer software on a subject with the other materials in that subject.

   Oregon Trail (a simulated trek across the plains). Class with other materials on the Oregon Trail in 978.

   Operation Frog (shows how to dissect a frog). Class with other materials on frog anatomy in 591.4.

Story Tree (a mechanical assist to writing fiction). Class with other materials on writing fiction in 808.3.

2. If several computer software programs unrelated in topic or interdisciplinary in nature are on the same disk, then classify the collection in 005.3 (Computer programs).

"Microzine" (a computer program "periodical" containing many programs in each issue). Class in 005.3.

but

"MECC Social Studies Disk" (numerous programs, all of a political science nature) should be classed in 320.

3. If the software or book material describes computers in general, computer hardware, or computer systems, class in the following:

004   Data processing   Computer science
      (class materials on computer literacy here)
004.1   General works on specific types of computers
004.7   Peripherals

005   Computer programming, programs, data
005.1   Programming
005.2   Programming for specific types of computers (arrange by computer brand, using brand name like author letters below the Dewey number) Example: programming for the Apple: 005.2 A
005.3   Programs
      (general interdisciplinary programs or collections of programs on many topics)
005.4   Systems programming and programs
      (operating systems such as DOS or proDOS or PCDOS go here)
005.7   Data in computer systems
      (general purpose databases or database programs such as "PFS File" go here)

006   Special computer methods
006.3   Artificial intelligence
006.5   Computer sound synthesis
006.6   Computer graphics (programs such as "Dazzel Draw" go here)

4. Class computer engineering in 621.39
5. Avoid the innocuous 372 classification for computer teaching materials.

The following samples are from three software programs; their main entry cards prepared for both level 1 (figure 4a) and level 2 (figure 4b) description.

Example 1: *Information taken from the first few computer screens when the program is booted*

Nutri-calc™
Dietary Nutritional Analysis System

Nutri-calc DNAS is a powerful tool designed to aid in managing diets for any number of people. It consists of several programs. The first, Nutri-calc, calculates the nutrient intake for an individual based on the foods consumed. The second, Calorie™, computes the ideal caloric intake of each person based on age, sex, desired weight goal, and activity level.

Menu on the second screen:
Nutri-calc
Calorie
Disk Backup
Change Nutrient Names
System Shutdown

Cover and guide title: Nutri-calc™

Disk labels:
PCD Systems Inc.	PCD Systems Inc.
Nutri-Calc	Nutri-Calc
c1981	c1981
System disk	Data disk

FIGURE 4a. Brief cataloging (level 1)

Computer program

641.1   Nutri-calc : dietary nutritional analysis system. — PCD Systems,
N   c1981.
        2 computer disks (Apple II+) + 1 manual.

        Printer optional.
        Contents: Nutri-calc — Calorie.

        1. Nutrition.   I. Title: Calorie.

FIGURE 4b.   Catalog card (level 2)

641.1 N	Nutri-calc [machine-readable data file] : dietary nutritional analysis system. — [Penn Yan, N.Y.] : PCD Systems, c1981. 2 computer disks (Apple II+) ; 5¼ in. + 1 manual (49 p. ; 28 cm.), in binder. Manual for version 2.2, c1979. Printer optional. Summary: Calculates total nutritional intake and average daily intake for a 1- to 7-day period, as well as the ideal caloric intake. Contents: Nutri-calc — Calorie. 1. Nutrition. I. Title: Dietary nutritional analysis system. II. Title: Calorie.

Notes on decisions

1. *Nutri-calc* seems to be the title proper, as well as the title of the first program on the disk.
2. Use of the GMD is optional. The GMD might be used above the call number instead of some code devised for audiovisual media.
3. The place of publication is given in brackets because it had to be researched; it was not anywhere on the material.
4. There was no version number on the program disk, but ''manual version'' and early copyright date lead one to believe that this program is a later version than 2.2.
5. The summary was taken from information on the title screen and in the manual.

Example 2:   *Information from title screen*

ALPHA PLOT

by Bert Kersey and Jack Cassidy

copyright c1982

Beagle Brothers Micro Software
4315 Sierra Vista
San Diego, CA 92103

Disk label:

> *Alpha Plot*
> by Bert Kersey and Jack Cassidy
> c1982, Beagle Bros. Micro Software
> 4315 Sierra Vista, San Diego, CA 92103
> (714) 296-6400

Documentation cover page:

Alpha Plot
Hi-Res Apple Graphics/Text Utility
by Bert Kersey and Jack Cassidy
Unlocked and Unprotected
Compatible with
—Apple IIe
—Apple II+
—Apple II

2nd documentation cover page:

Beagle Bros. presents
Apple Tip Book #4
A New Assortment of
Apple II Tips and Tricks

Plus Complete Instructions for Using Alpha Plot
Hi-Res Text/Graphics Utility
by Bert Kersey and Jack Cassidy

Entire contents copyright 1982,
Beagle Bros. Micro Software

Notes on decisions

1. The Beagle Brothers documentation manuals usually follow the same format. This one is entitled Apple Tip Book #4, and the manual ends with instructions for the utility disk. Programmers are often as interested in the tip book as they are in the program on the utility disk; thus the necessity to trace the tip book title.
2. The program is written by two well-known programmers; thus the choice of main entry similar to dual authorship of a book.

FIGURE 5a.   Brief Cataloging (level 1)

Computer program

006.6	Kersey, Burt.
K	Alpha plot / by Burt Kersey and Jack Cassidy. — Beagle Brothers, c1982.
	1 computer disk (Apple IIe, II+, II) + 1 manual + 1 keyboard chart + 1 peeks and pokes chart.
	Manual title: Beagle Bros. presents Apple tip book #4.
	1. Computer graphics. I. Cassidy Jack. II. Title. III. Title: Apple tip book #4.

FIGURE 5b. Cataloging Card (level 2)

006.6   Kersey, Burt.
K   Alpha plot [machine-readable data file] / by Burt Kersey and Jack
Cassidy. — San Diego, Calif. : Beagle Brothers, c1982.
1 computer disk (Apple IIe, II+, II) ; 5¼ in. + 1 manual (17 p. ;
25 cm.), in plastic slipcase + 1 keyboard chart + 1 peeks and pokes
chart.

       Manual title: Beagle Bros. presents Apple tip book #4 : a new
assortment of Apple II tips and tricks, plus complete instructions for
using Alpha plot hi-res text/graphics utility.
       Summary: A utility useful in creating high resolution graphics with
text characters.

       1. Computer graphics.   I. Cassidy, Jack.   II. Beagle
Brothers Micro Software.   III. Title.   IV. Title: Beagle Bros.
presents Apple II tip book #4.   V. Title: Apple tip book #4.

Example 3: *Information taken from the first few computer screens when the
program is booted*

Social Studies
Volume 1
Version 4.3
c1980

Menu:
Crimex
Elect1
Elect2
Elect3
Energy
Limits
Future
Policy
USPop
Cleanup

Disk labels:

MECC
c1980
DOS 3.3
Social Studies
Volume 1
Version 4.3

Information from guide:

CRIMEX:	This program simulates crime-control in a large city.
ELECT1:	This program simulates presidential elections of the 19th century.
ELECT2:	This program simulates presidential elections of the 20th century.
ELECT3:	This program simulates presidential elections based on factors entered by the user.
ENERGY:	This program is a simulation in which the user makes energy-related decisions.
FUTURE:	This program is a simulation which shows the possible effects various decisions have on energy supplies.
LIMITS:	This program is a simulation based on the book Limits to Growth.
POLICY:	This program simulates the impact special interest groups have on policy formation.
USPOP:	This program projects the U.S. population based on user-determined parameters.
CLEANUP:	This program allows you to delete old files that were created with the ELECT3 and POLICY programs.

Notes on decisions

1. Both main entries show title analytics requiring 10 cards in addition to main entry, shelflist and 3 subject cards. Analytics are important in this case. Surely, a teacher or student will need one of the programs on the disk and won't know what disk it is on.
2. The Dewey number is very broad—a catchall.

FIGURE 6a.   Brief Cataloging (level 1)

Computer program

320   Social studies, volume 1. — Version 4.3 — MECC, c1980.
S   2 computer disks (Apple II) + 2 manuals.

             Some programs require use of a printer. Limits requires a color
             monitor for graphs.
                 Contents: Crimex — Elect1 — Elect2 — Elect3 — Energy —
             Limits — Future — Policy — USPop — Cleanup.

                 1. Elections — United States.   2. Political science.
             3. Population.   I. Title analytics.

FIGURE 6b.   Catalog card (level 2)

320   Social studies, volume 1 [machine-readable data file]. — Version 4.3.
S   — [St. Paul, Minn.]
           : Minnesota Educational Computing Consortium, c1980.
           2 computer disks (Apple II +) ; 5¹/₄ in. + 2 manuals (53 p. , 101
           p. ; 29 cm.).
               Some programs require use of a printer.   Limits requires a color
           monitor for graphs.
               Contents: Crimex — Elect1 — Elect2 — Elect3 — Energy —
           Limits — Future — Policy — USPop — Cleanup.
 	
           1. Elections — United States.   2. Political science.
           3. Population.   I. Title analytics.

Storage and Retrieval

The care of microcomputer software presents a number of challenges to the library media center staff. Neglect of certain factors can have a disastrous effect. A few basic rules governing the care of disks and microcomputer cassette tapes will help preserve their usefulness.

1. Protect disks from dust. Keep them in their jackets and in closed containers when they are not in use. Dust and hair can easily damage a disk so that it cannot be read by the microcomputer.
2. Keep disks and tapes away from magnetic surfaces. For example, don't lay them on the disk drive, graphics tablets, or other static-electricity–charged surfaces which may erase them.
3. While most electronic detection systems will not erase microcomputer disks or tapes, the demagnetizing devices for books and other materials will. Alert the staff to this fact.
4. Whenever possible, have students use one copy of the program and keep another backup copy in storage to use in case of emergency.
5. Computer disks should not be folded, bent, heated, squeezed, sat on, exposed to the heat of the sun, carried in pockets, chewed by dogs, or used as Frisbees. Such treatment usually results in a blank microcomputer screen.
6. Static electricity can destroy disks.

Microcomputer disks are not as tolerant to slight damage as other audiovisual materials. A filmstrip can be scratched but still be shown; a transparency can be yellowed but still be usable. An audiotape can be spliced, but a damaged microcomputer disk is unusable. This means that extra precautions are in order if instruction is not to be interrupted by machine failure.

Backup disks are best kept in dust-proof cabinets or storage boxes. A number of types are available from commercial vendors. Looseleaf notebook pages made of plastic which store two disks are also easy to use and help protect the original disk. Keep the disk away from the notebook rings.

Software that is to be used by students can be stored on regular shelves in dust-proof packaging, with the accompanying documentation. The problem of storing several pieces in a single box is the same with microcomputer software as it is with sound filmstrips and media kits. Every piece must be labeled and accounted for during the circulation process. If a list of package contents is typed on the book pocket, the circulation clerk can check the list against the package when the material is circulated and again when it is returned. If the system requirements are added to the note on the book pocket, the user always has a convenient source of information for the type of computer, peripherals, or other requirements for that particular program.

Paperclips should not be used in any package of software. If they have been kept in a magnetized paperclip holder, they could cause glitches on the disks. Double layers of labels on disks may get caught in disk drives. There are types of markers on the market that will mark directly and permanently on the disk covers, eliminating the need for a label entirely.

If the manufacturer does not provide a backup disk for each disk purchased, the library media specialist may wish to create a backup disk in the library media center. Such a procedure is legal since purchasers are entitled to a single backup of every computer program purchased. However, the copying of commercially protected software may be a problem. Programs have been created to break into such protection systems to access a disk. Such programs should be used within the constraints of the copyright law.

As with other audiovisual materials, microcomputer software may need to be packaged (if locally developed) or repackaged to fit into local storage facilities. A number of library-supply jobbers carry a wide variety of storage supplies such as boxes, labels, notebooks, and plastic storage pages.

Most manufacturers have a policy for replacement of damaged software at no charge or at cost. Usually the original disk must be returned to the company as evidence of purchase. In case of loss, proof of purchase may facilitate inexpensive replacement.

Several factors may cause microcomputer programs to fail. Electrical power surges can destroy both equipment and software almost instantaneously. Disk drives which are reading too slowly or too fast may not load programs. A simple speed adjustment of the drive is needed regularly. When a problem arises, do not jump to the conclusion that the software is at fault. Connections may be loose, boards in the computer can become corroded, and microchips can work loose from their sockets. Library media specialists can usually solve the problems, thus adding to the life of the software and to the success of the users.

Electronic Mail

Doris Epler

Mail stored in electronic mailboxes . . . It sounds like Space Age talk; and indeed, just like the space shuttle, it is an activity whose time has come. The Federal Communications Commission defines electronic mail as "the sending and receiving of messages which otherwise would be done via the Postal Service or the telephone."[1] In a study conducted by the Pennsylvania Department of Education in 1981, electronic mail was defined as "any method which electronically transmits information from a sender to a receiver in the form of a message."[2] John Callahan, research director of Information Technology Research, defines electronic mail as "the substitution of the transmission of electronic impulses for the physical transportation of documents."[3] The key characteristic of electronic mail is to move information rather than paper. It is a means of communication between people, not places. Since users may access their mail wherever they happen to be, it is insensitive to geography.[4]

The technology of electronic mail has a history of more than 100 years but has been used as a tool for business communications for fewer than 25 years. In the early nineteenth century, the telegraph provided a means of sending messages electronically, but it was limited since the messages were in Morse Code and could only be transmitted to the other end of the telegraph wire. Teletypewriters, which appeared on the scene in the early twentieth century, permitted messages to

---

[1]Robert J. Veenstra, "Electronic Mail Has a Future in the Library," *Special Libraries* 72 (October 1981): 338.

[2]Bureau of Information Systems, Pennsylvania Department of Education, "Electronic Mail Study" (November 1981).

[3]John Callahan, "Electronic Mail Will Be the Critical Pipeline," *The Office* 95 (January 1982): 98–99.

[4]Ian P. Sharp, "The Impact of Electronic Mail on Management Functions," *Business Quarterly* 46 (Summer 1981): 81–83.

be sent in keyboard characters, but the receiver had to be ready to accept the message or communication could not occur. Early computers could store messages and forward them to a receiver. But it was not until the early 1970s that computer-based message systems (CBMS) became a reality. The electronic technology and communication facilities that were available some years ago now make electronic mail possible. CBMS is the result of work done by the time-sharing service industry, computer networks, and Advanced Research Projects Agency. This new phenomenon, less than a decade old, uses the computer as an integral component of human communications.[5]

CBMS can receive, store, or transmit messages, using electronic mailboxes, and integrates the three technologies of word processing, computer networking, and database management.

Word processing assists the terminal user in message composition, computer networking aids in the message delivery, and database management provides for the storage and retrieval of mail in electronic mailboxes.[6]

When school library media specialists need to communicate with someone, they generally use the telephone, the postal system, or a face-to-face meeting. Each of these well-accepted methods of exchanging information forces certain restrictions on the effective and efficient use of valuable resources, and each plays a role in the day-to-day operations of school library media centers. The telephone companies now offer such technological advances as teleconferencing, call forwarding, and message recorders. The postal system now can provide overnight delivery of mail. And airlines help to get people to distant meeting sites much more rapidly than automobiles. Each of these methods of communication has advantages, but the primary reason why library media specialists should use electronic mail is that information itself has become more valuable.

Electronic mail permits a user to send a message to one receiver, several recipients, or a whole group of people by inputting the information only one time. Sending a message to a group is as easy as sending it to one individual.

A decision to get involved in electronic mail should not be made just to get into the computer race. The *reasons* must be clear and well defined before plans are made to implement such a system. Therefore, both the benefits and the impact of electronic mail should be carefully examined before equipment and services are purchased. Electronic mail outlays should be *investments* which are part of a long-range technology plan. The full benefits of electronic mail technology can only be realized by carefully leveraging the technologies in order to prevent costly "electronic chaos" in the future.[7]

---

[5]Datapro Research Corporation, "Planning for Electronic Mail" (Delran, N.J., July 1980), pp. C520–610–101–5.

[6]"Electronic Mail Study," p. 7, and Walter E. Ulrich, "Assets of Electronic Mail Far Exceed the Liabilities," *The Office* 96 (November 1982): 152–62, 202.

[7]Ulrich, "Assets of Electronic Mail . . . ."

Equipment

Computer mail stations take a variety of forms. A microcomputer or a terminal is needed, as well as some type of interface or modem, to permit access to the telephone lines. A printer permits hard copies of messages to be made and is a definite asset to an electronic mail system. If a microcomputer is used to implement an electronic mail system, it does not mean that it is dedicated to just this function. This same system, if placed in a school library media center, can be used to search for information stored in computerized databases, to perform various types of library management, and to help students build information processing skills through computer-assisted instruction.

Message Transmittal

Certain conditions must exist before messages can be sent by electronic mail. First, both the sender and the receiver must have access to the same CBMS. In most situations involving schools, this means that a microcomputer or terminal with interfacing has access to a large computer owned by a commercial vendor of online services. Several excellent firms offer electronic mail to their clients, and these are discussed in detail later in this section. Second, the sender must know the "t" number of the receiver, which provides access to the receiver in much the same way as a telephone number.

The procedures necessary to send a message are fairly simple:

1. The sender "signs on" to the system, identifying himself or herself with a password. The computer then checks its memory, to determine if the password is valid, before it performs any services. (This is much the same way that electronic banking is conducted.) If an incorrect password is entered into the system, access to all services is prohibited.
2. The sender types the "t" number of the receiver and inputs the message into the system. The computer stores this message in its memory, the electronic mailbox.
3. As users activate their systems, the computer constantly checks the electronic mailbox to determine if there are messages for those particular users. If a user's "t" number matches a "t" number in the electronic mailbox, the computer notifies the user that a message is pending.
4. The user can then choose to read the message or ignore it.
5. Other options are available to the user who receives a message: make a hard copy of the message, store it electronically on a disk, or send it to another member of the system.
6. The receiver also has the option of editing the message, or adding comments, before sending it to another member.

It must be noted, however, that, if a user does not turn the computer on and read the messages, they will reside in the electronic mailbox until the time period for holding messages in that CBMS expires. Users of electronic mail systems must check their mailboxes frequently, or a message will become outdated and ineffective. The human attention paid to this system will contribute significantly to the success or failure of such a venture.

Benefits of Electronic Mail

Speed. Electronic mail has the speed that enables communication to take place instantly. It increases the timeliness of message content and improves its effectiveness by permitting the receiver to have immediate access to the communication. Managerial productivity increases through the sheer speed in which something can happen. In addition, the same message can be sent to multiple receivers and has to be entered into the system only one time. Electronic technology is such a powerful tool that it allows librarians to reach the site of many information needs without leaving their seats.[8]

Reduction of Turnaround Time. Electronic mail permits the user to respond to messages immediately and forward answers to other users. If users check their mailboxes frequently, messages can be responded to in a few hours, or minutes, or even instantly! It overcomes the problems of trying to communicate across time zones and helps to reduce the time people spend discussing things like the weather.

Flexibility. CBMS permits the receiver to scan the messages in the mailbox, read all the messages or only selected ones, print the messages needed in hard copy, or store the messages for retrieval later. This permits flexibility, since the receiver has control over which messages to read and which to ignore. The ease with which messages can be sent and received can open communication lines between the point of origination of the message and the points to which the message will be sent. Electronic mail can provide instant feedback, as dialog occurs between the sender and the receiver.

Reduction of Clerical Work. Nonelectronic communications are often delayed because messages are stacked on someone's desk, waiting to be typed. Electronic mail can reduce this backlog since messages can be sent by any staff member in a quick and effective manner. With minimal training, anyone can utilize an electronic mail system. This will reduce the load of clerical work since electronic messages do not have to be folded and inserted into envelopes, and copies are not hand filed. All the procedures for recording and storing messages can be handled by the CBMS.

Reduction of Educational Isolation. For school library media specialists, one of the most important features of electronic mail is that it reduces educational iso-

---

[8]William F. Wright and Donald T. Hawkins, "Information Technology, a Bibliography," *Special Libraries* 72 (April 1981): 163–74.

lation. The structure of the educational system sometimes inhibits communication by virtue of its size. When communications are sent, they are often locked into one system after another. This sometimes causes information to be so late as to be meaningless, and in some cases, the intended receiver never gets the message at all. School library media specialists could have instant access to one another, as well as to regional or intermediate units, the state department of education, and other librarians throughout the United States. The potential of such a network is tremendous and is limited only by individual motivation and creativity.

Cost Effectiveness. Sending messages electronically is generally very cost effective. The time spent on incompleted telephone calls and performing various clerical tasks in nonelectronic message sending can be saved by using an electronic mail system to handle some of the communications.

> Electronic mail can displace the costs of other communications and reduce less productive salary dollars. It makes people more productive and can hasten the analysis and dissemination of information. That means faster and better decisions, and better performance.[9]

The key to achieving cost effectiveness in an electronic mail system for a school library media center, however, is that this activity is secondary to a need which is even more directly related to library media service: the provision of reference services. School library media centers which are facing budgetary cuts or no-growth financial patterns can greatly increase the number of references available to their students and teachers by contracting with a commercial vendor to search computerized databases for information. Electronic mail, in some instances, will also be available, but will not be the primary objective in using an electronic system.

Cost savings, however, may not be the primary benefit from electronic mail. The typical school library media specialist is overworked and short of time. Electronic mail will provide some relief by enabling this specialist to organize communications better.

Expanded Information Sources. Library media specialists can also use CBMS to seek references and resources from other libraries. This can be done within a school system, a regional center or intermediate unit, or across a state. It can also include multiple types of libraries, such as public, community colleges, universities, private and parochial schools, and business and industries. Such a system will enable staff in each library to let their needs be known, and staff in other libraries can then choose whether to respond to those needs.

Reduction of Forms. Electronic mail has the capability of reducing the number of forms to which schools must respond. Many statistical items needed by state departments of education or regional and intermediate units can be transmitted electronically.

---

[9]Ulrich, "Assets of Electronic Mail . . . ," p. 202.

Management Tool. The real strength of electronic mail lies in its ability to provide libraries with all the information it needs about everything that is happening everywhere, what other librarians are thinking, and up-to-date accounts of decision-making processes. All of this can be accomplished without recourse to the telephone or attendance at meetings.

Problems

Electronic mail systems can be misused if they are not monitored properly. Just as library media specialists are inundated with "junk mail," the electronic mailbox will generate the same type of communications if messages are not properly tailored. Messages need to be succinct but understandable, and meaningful to the receiver, if electronic mail is to be fully utilized and cost effective.

No matter how many messages need to be sent, if the receiver does not have the capability of receiving electronic messages, the system will not survive. There must be enough people with access to the same CBMS to make the system worthwhile. Proper management is also needed so that messages will not be unnecessarily duplicated, since many staff members may be sending messages to the same target audience. Audit trails of communications will be lost if messages are not saved and stored properly.

Consideration must be given to several areas before a decision can be made to get involved in an electronic mail system:

Cost. The cost of start-up equipment must be determined accurately. Some library media specialists already have equipment in place, much of which was purchased by Title IVB funds. However, advice should be sought through regional centers or intermediate units, the state department of education, or regional informational centers to be certain that the equipment being considered can perform the desired services. In some cases, adjustments or additional peripherals are needed to make the system function properly. Monies must also be allocated to pay any membership fees, online searches, royalty fees, or telecommunication charges. The equipment will require preventive maintenance or, perhaps, replacement parts.

Excitement about the potential of electronic mail should not cloud the financial considerations. However, in most cases the cost can be justified if proper data is collected on nonelectronic communication charges and compared with the projected costs of communicating electronically.

Training. If the system will be fully utilized—that is, database searching, electronic mail, and library management—extensive training must be provided. If only the electronic mail component will be implemented, most people can be trained to use such a system effectively in a few hours.

Human Element. Most adults are not as comfortable with computers as children are. Consideration must be given to "fear of the unknown" and the desire to keep things as they are. Technological change can be a frightening experience, or it can be highly motivating and exciting. It all depends on the approach by decision makers to get people involved and interested in electronic mail. If it is viewed as a fad or novelty, the venture will be doomed to failure. Library media specialists should facilitate the dissemination of information within their schools, and the use of technology to handle mundane activities will enable them to direct their talents toward enhancing the image of their media center.[10]

Some librarians fear that they will become obsolete if information becomes so readily available to others electronically. Library media specialists must be encouraged to become familiar with technology so that they can serve as full-time readers' advisers and provide reassuring human contact for those who fear isolation when they work with machines.[11] From simple operations such as electronic mail to more complex activities such as database searching, the human element must be of primary consideration. CBMS cannot succeed if this component is ignored or not addressed properly.

Justification. In this day and age of budgetary constraints, any new ideas which mean spending scarce dollars must be justified. Therefore, decision makers need to be made aware of the many benefits electronic mail can provide. Very often, however, electronic mail can ride on the coattails of a project with greater visible impact on school library media centers, such as technology for library management or information retrieval. The financial strain at the top of the library budget for activities such as acquisition, circulation, cataloging, and researching will continue to decrease as technology improves. Justification becomes more meaningful if the reasons for wanting to utilize electronic mail can be directly linked to the goals and objectives of the school library media curriculum.

Target Audience. The population to be served by the electronic mail system needs to be defined. Will the service include students? Teachers? Administrators? Community members? Must the target audience be heterogeneous or homogeneous in makeup? Will there be enough members in the system to provide efficient and effective service to senders and receivers? While electronic mail has enormous potential, the system will be weakened if only a small number of subscribers can communicate with one another.[12] Before contracting with a vendor for electronic mail service, schools should be certain that they will have access to those with whom they wish to communicate.

Technology. While the technology is available to send messages of various length to multiple receivers, the form of the CBMS places limitations on its use. Consideration must be given to the number of areas which can be reached at one

---

[10]"1985: New Technologies for Libraries," *Library Journal* 105 (July 1980): 1473–78.
[11]Susan Spaeth Cherry, "Special Report: Electronic Library Association Born at Columbus Forum," *American Libraries* 12 (May 1981): 275–76.
[12]Frank Reardon et al., *Evaluation Report: PENN*LINK Pilot Program*, Pennsylvania Department of Education, February 18, 1983.

time and the acceptable length of messages before contracts are signed with a commercial vendor for electronic mail service. A clear understanding of the limitations of the CBMS, upfront, will avoid pitfalls as the system is implemented.

Some schools have access to large mainframes which handle recordkeeping for the district. It is sometimes possible, in these cases, to use excess central processing space and storage capacity to permit internal applications such as electronic mail.[13] While this will help to solve some of the problems of communicating within the district, it inhibits information flow outside the immediate area.

Role of the School Library Media Specialist

The role of the school library media specialist will *in no way* be diminished by the services available through electronic mail. In fact, the role will be greatly enhanced since the CBMS will serve the needs of students, teachers, and administrators. Electronic systems can contribute toward strengthening the role of the library media specialist as a manager in gathering, collating, and arranging information. The librarian can also use electronic systems to teach students to use technology for information retrieval.

School library media uses of electronic mail are:

Enhancement of Curriculum. In addition to managing the resources of the media center, most library media specialists are also responsible for teaching library media skills. They have a responsibility to assist students in the development of information processing skills which they will need in lifelong learning. Therefore, the curriculum must reflect current trends and technology for information retrieval. Before electronic mail becomes part of the school library media center, an upfront decision should be made regarding how this technology can be integrated into the school library media curriculum.

Interlibrary Loan. Electronic mail messages can be sent to members on the system to seek resources. This can be done, within a geographical area between different types of libraries or across boundary lines with similar types of libraries, providing such networking arrangements have been made.

Rush Requests. There are times when people within the school system need information immediately. Electronic mail provides the speed to handle rush requests.

Hotline Information. Information which is ''hot off the press'' can be shared rapidly. This enables multiple receivers to learn new information, all at the same time.

Conference Planning. Multiple users can plan conferences over the electronic mail system. This reduces the need for meetings and saves valuable time.

---

[13]A. J. Wright, ''After the Fall: The Use of Surplus Capacity in an Academic Library Automation System,'' April 26, 1981 (ED 220 099, mf).

Ordering Supplies. In some cases, orders for books and supplies can be forwarded to vendors, if they are members of the same CBMS.

Future Uses. CBMS users can *download* software programs into their system and transfer articles, papers, and even chapters of books.

One of the best ways to experiment with some of these applications is for the library media specialist to connect into a local electronic bulletin board. Almost every city of any size now has a network of computer hobbyists who dial one microcomputer and share all kinds of news, tips, and electronic mail, and even download programs. All that is needed to experiment is a microcomputer, a modem, and a telephone line. To locate existing bulletin boards, contact local computer clubs for the telephone numbers and available hours. Several months of sharing messages back and forth will provide enough experience so that one will be able to set up a *local library* bulletin board. Local bulletin boards may develop into regional, state, or even national bulletin boards.

Computer-Based Message Systems

Many commercial firms and state and national agencies provide electronic mail service. The motivation behind choosing one over the other should be whether or not the system will permit the purchaser to perform the functions desired with the appropriate target audience. Those which are particularly applicable for electronic mail service for school library media centers are as follows:

Bibliographic Retrieval Services (BRS) provides electronic mail service and access to over 60 computerized databases, many of which contain educational information. Educational institutions which contract with BRS are automatically members of the School Practices Information Network (SPIN). This network permits electronic access to all members of SPIN, provides reduced searching rates to all members, and allows access to the School Practices Information File (SPIF). This file contains data about school practices that are being implemented throughout the United States. BRS's target audience is the researcher, both student and professional. New users need special training before going online.

CompuServe offers a large number of online services which are aimed at a wide target audience. For example, it has national and international news wires; financial information on thousands of securities, stocks as well as bonds; electronic bulletin boards; a full-text, electronic version of *Academic American Encyclopedia*; and of course electronic mail—to name a few. It is a menu-driven system; so the new user needs no special training before going online.

The SOURCE, like CompuServe, is aimed at a wide target audience. It provides information in education, business, government, news, and sports. It too offers electronic mail. Again like CompuServe, it is a menu-driven system; so the new user needs no special training before going online.

Linking Information Needs: Technology-Education-Libraries (LIN-TEL), a pilot network, is sponsored by the Pennsylvania Department of Education, the Bureau of the State Library, and the School Library Media Division. Its 75 member sites include school library media centers, intermediate units, public libraries, a community college, two institutions of higher education, a private school, and several parochial schools. It provides network members with access to computerized databases and electronic mail services through BRS.

PENN*LINK, a network of over 90 members, is part of the Pennsylvania Department of Education's experiment in technology. It utilizes The SOURCE as its CBMS to provide electronic mail service to its members. In addition, PENN* LINK members have access to all of the databases in The SOURCE.

The Future

In the next decade, electronic mail is likely to become a standard method of communication in both the home and the workplace. At the moment, it appears that numerous forms of communication will be available in the future which will either accompany or replace the present-day telephone and postal services. Futurists predict that over 30 billion pieces of information will be electronically delivered by the year 2000. When voice transmission is added to electronic mail, telephone usage will change radically.

Electronic mail in school library media centers is already a reality in some Pennsylvania schools. Library media specialists need to pioneer in adopting this technology as a new form of information transfer, or it will be a function of the school office. Opportunities to locate, find, share, and create information-gathering and -dissemination processes are staggering. The challenge is to be ready.

PART THREE

SERVICES OF THE FACILITY

Traditionally, services in the school library media center have reflected the trends in education. As curriculum evolved, the media center collection and services were planned to meet student and faculty needs. When teachers used the lecture method exclusively, a small reference collection was sufficient. As methods of teaching changed to incorporate media into the classroom, films, filmstrips, records, and multimedia kits became necessary items in the media center holdings.

The introduction of microcomputers into the media center gives services a new dimension. The expanded sources of reference to include online databases will expand the capabilities of the school library media center to meet the information needs of the clientele. A new medium, the interactive videodisc, stores more records than has been possible in the past, and the microcomputer permits easy, rapid access to these records.

One of the possibilities of the videodisc storage capabilities is the use of this medium to learn of the holdings of other libraries in the immediate area or in the nation. Library media specialists have been borrowing materials from the nearby public and academic libraries for half a century. Access to these collections was limited when there was little knowledge of the materials available. Using the videodisc and communications programs on the microcomputer is opening the resources of other libraries to students in schools.

Finally, the teaching of programming to students may be a responsibility of staff in the library media center. The final paper explains one curriculum designed to accomplish this.

Electronic Information

Christopher C. Swisher and
Jacqueline Mancall

If their library media specialist has a microcomputer, a telephone, and a modem, students may be placed in closer contact with the vast information world in which they live. Millions of items of information, stored in central computers, will be at their beck and call. Electronic information services and networks allow students to locate answers to reference questions; perform bibliographic searches; send messages electronically; locate market reports, employment services, even movie reviews; and engage in electronic games and drills. The expression "Let your fingers do the walking" was never more appropriate, as everyone from professional information managers to school children are accessing bibliographic data banks, stock market quotations, electronic community bulletin boards, full-text electronic newspapers, and more. The Apple, Atari, TRS-80, and Commodore microcomputers can be configured to access virtually unlimited information resources, as well as send messages.

The major advantages of engaging in an electronic dialog for information can be summed up in two words: selectability and convenience. Instead of the physical resources of only one library media center, literally millions of resources become part of the students' information storehouse; and instead of moving from one source to another (perhaps even from one library to another), the trained electronic searcher can direct the computer to perform a search or answer a question.

The most widely discussed example of this is the computerized bibliographic search, in which students locate records of online materials that are pertinent to their school-related needs. The trained student-searcher employs a set of predefined commands to direct a computer to search machine-readable indexes for references. The searcher engages, in effect, in an interactive dialog, and develops the ability to review responses to an inquiry and modify and revise a search as it progresses. There are snags, of course, in this picture of Utopia. Many of the references retrieved online may be to materials either too sophisticated or too unique to be readily available. The advantages, however, are equally obvious. The search is quicker than one done manually; the available information is more up to date; the search can be more comprehensive; and—as importantly—excitement is generated about the research process.

Schools can subscribe to a wide variety of information utilities that will provide, for a fee, information on many subjects, as well as allow students to send messages and create files electronically. Databases have been created by many types of organizations and cover diverse subject areas. These producers include government agencies as well as nonprofit and for-profit organizations. Although some databases can be searched by making arrangements directly with their producers, it is more common to purchase access through database vendors, since they have large computers that make a wide variety of databases and services available to many users simultaneously.

There is, of course, another reason for introducing electronic information services at the student level: the school's responsibility to prepare the student to become a competent member of society. Public recognition has been given to the growing importance of information and information access in the modern world. Those who understand and can manipulate the tools of information retrieval will be better prepared than those who cannot and, therefore, may be more successful.

Online information sources are as varied as the books, periodicals, audiovisual media, indexes, encyclopedias, and newspapers in your media center. Moreover, electronic or *dial-up* information sources can be broken down into several categories: bibliographic databases, library resource networks, information utilities, electronic newspapers, and electronic encyclopedias. Each is discussed in detail below.

Bibliographic Databases

Access to bibliographic data can be provided by large companies, such as Dialog and BRS (Bibliographic Retrieval Services), as well as by the lesser-known System Development Corporation's Orbit and numerous smaller bibliographic services. The two companies that are of greatest interest to school library media specialists are Dialog and BRS.

Lockheed's vast information network, known as Dialog Information Services, is located in Palo Alto, California. Dialog service includes over 175 databases, covering such diverse areas as humanities, current affairs, science, technology, business, social science, and medicine. Among the databases supplied by Dialog that are of particular interest to students are America: History and Life, which covers the full range of U.S. and Canadian history and current affairs; Book Review Index, a reference guide for locating published reviews of books and periodical titles; ERIC, the complete database on educational materials; Magazine Index, an online database which offers broad coverage of general-interest magazines; National Newspaper Index, which provides complete indexing of the *New York Times*, the *Wall Street Journal*, the *Washington Post*, and other newspapers of national reputation; and Newsearch, a daily-updated index of the nation's leading newspapers, magazines, and periodicals. Students whose school library media centers are Dialog subscribers also have access to complete bibliographic records of all materials cataloged by the Library of Congress through the LC MARC database.

Dialog is a fairly straightforward system. Basic search commands are easily mastered. Records can be searched by controlled vocabulary (thesaurus) terminology or by free-text terms. Search results can be printed directly on a terminal or requested from Dialog's printer, to be mailed the next day from California. Many documents indexed in Dialog's databases can be ordered through Dialog directly through your terminal.

In addition, Dialog offers a special rate, available to educational users through their Classroom Instruction Program, that permits users in schools to access most of the Dialog databases for $15 per hour. The cost of typical database access ranges from $25 to $100 per hour. At the $15 per hour rate, a student's 10- to 15-minute interaction with the computer network will cost about $3. Of course, some limitations are placed on access at this rate that prevent users from taking advantage of full-system possibilities. These do not, however, outweigh the tremendous cost savings available through the Classroom Instruction Program.

Bibliographic Retrieval Services (BRS), in Latham, New York, provides more than 80 databases, covering humanities, social sciences, life and physical sciences, and business. It is second only to Dialog in the breadth of information it makes available. BRS is unique among database vendors because of the sophistication and power of its search language, which incorporates all the standard features of other systems, such as Dialog, as well as many unique capabilities.

In addition to the standard Boolean logic operators, BRS subscribers can use word-root searches, limit searches to specific record fields (title, abstract, and others), and conduct a unique cross-database search. BRS also allows the merging of products of different database searches into one printout.

Among the databases provided by BRS which will be of interest to students are Disc, a microcomputer literature database; The Academic American Encyclopedia; RICE (Resources in Computer Education), which covers state-of-the-art computer applications in the schools, software producers, and educational courseware/software; and MSGS, an electronic message service. An additional database, The National College Databank, will provide prospective students, counselors, and administrators with comparative data on U.S. and Canadian colleges and universities. This new database, produced by Peterson's Guides, lists college name, size, enrollment, admissions data, academic emphasis, and financial aid information.

Like Dialog, BRS has an Educational Online Training Program which may be made available to school library media centers. The costs for *online connect time* range from $14 to $16 per hour. BRS provides free training to educators involved in this program.

A recent trend in the vending of information online is after-hours availability of specially designed, low-cost, information networks, tailored for home microcomputer users. None of these networks can be accessed during school hours, but they are, nonetheless, of interest to school library media specialists. Knowledge Index, a subset of Dialog's online databases, uses simplified search procedures and specializes in the kind of magazine, journal, and newspaper literature that appeals to school-age researchers.

Likewise, in an effort to woo home microcomputer users, BRS offers its BRS After Dark home computer service. In a simple, menu-driven format, more than 20 specially selected databases are made available at reduced rates. This service is available after 6 p.m. The educational community should lobby for school-hour availability of these easy-to-use, low-cost general-interest databases.

H. W. Wilson has also made its widely used indexes available online.[1] Its electronic information retrieval service, WilsonLine, which will eventually provide online access to all its indexes, became available to libraries and the public in October 1984. *Readers' Guide to Periodical Literature* can be accessed online. School library media specialists should be aware of this entry to the online market and consider the implications for its instructional programs.

Library Resource Networks

Several large, automated, library resource networks operate in the United States today, including Online Computer Library Center Inc. (OCLC) and Research Library Network (RLIN). While these bibliographic computer systems are designed to promote resource sharing among large academic, public, and research libraries, forward-thinking school library media specialists should be especially aware of OCLC, a system which boasts a number of schools among its membership.[2] OCLC is a network of over 3,300 member libraries which share an online union catalog of nearly 14 million records (1986). Participating libraries use the

---

[1]Carol Tenopir, "H. W. Wilson Online at Last," *Library Journal* 109 (September 1, 1984): 1616–17.
[2]Nancy Minnich, "Odysseus, Computers and an Integrated Library System," *Learning and Media* 11 (Summer 1983): 20.

OCLC online system to catalog all types of library materials, including books, serials, sound recordings, and audiovisual materials. Members also use the Interlibrary Loan Subsystem, Serials Control Subsystem, Acquisitions Subsystem, and the Name-Address Directory, which contain data about libraries, publishers, vendors, professional associations, and other organizations affiliated with the information industry. Most OCLC member libraries use dedicated terminals; however, OCLC encourages the use of microcomputers as terminals and began marketing an enhanced IBM PC early in 1984 for dial-up access. OCLC also plans to introduce an automated circulation system, based on the IBM personal computer.

The student whose library media center is a member of OCLC can find the location of any of the 14 million items in the database, and easily request the item by interlibrary loan. It may not be far-fetched to deduce that such students also benefit from accurately cataloged materials and an orderly card catalog, as well as a library media center staff that can spend more time on collection development and patron assistance and less time on original cataloging.

Information Utilities

Traditionally, utilities have provided consumers such services as telephone, water, and electricity. Now, a new kind of utility is making its presence known: the information utility. The Source, a subsidiary of *Reader's Digest*, is one example. It has 30,000 subscribers and is said to be adding 2,000 new subscribers per month.[3] CompuServe, the other principal information utility of interest to library media specialists, boasts 43,000 subscribers.

The Source, located in McLean, Virginia, offers a wide range of services, including communication, news, business, electronic bulletin boards, publishing, travel information, restaurant guides, and engineering computation. In fact, the Source is so comprehensive it is difficult to describe. Its user *interface* (computer jargon for the program with which a user interacts) is *menu driven*. At nearly every stage of a searcher's interaction, a list of options is presented on the screen, or at the printer, in "menu" form. Students simply select a number and the Source, through a series of steps, leads them to the information, program, or service of choice.

Students who have the Source available in their library media center will be interested in BASIC and Pascal programming languages, electronic games, consumer tips, and CompuStar, a national electronic shopping service. On the more serious side are Information on Demand, a literature search service, UPI News, and the Source's electronic "window" on events in Washington, D.C. Fees for all

[3]John Markoff and Tom Shea, "Information Utilities," *InfoWorld* 5 (March 28, 1983): 41.

of this range from $7.75 per hour during off-peak times to $29.75 per hour for prime-time access to the complete files of Source Plus.

Like the Source, CompuServe (in Columbus, Ohio) is a comprehensive potpourri of financial news, computer games, special-interest-group message boards, and information data banks for professionals. Students can access information on family life, Standard and Poor's commodities data bank, and a citizen's band simulator called CB. CompuServe's personal computing service also allows users to download various kinds of software (mostly games) into their own microcomputers for a fee. CompuServe, like most dial-up services, charges by connect time: $22.50 an hour during the day, $5 an hour in the evening. (Additional information, concerning these information utilities as electronic mail services, is given in the next section.)

Electronic Newspapers

The *New York Times*, the *Wall Street Journal*, and other newspapers of national significance have been indexed in printed form for quite some time. Now, major newspaper indexes are also becoming available online. These online indexes provide references in response to students' requests—after they have plowed through back issues on dusty shelves or in microform. However, a new type of newspaper access has evolved in recent years which may change the way newspaper references are searched and retrieved. One example is Vu-Text.

Vu-Text is a full-text database of articles from the *Philadelphia Inquirer,* the *Philadelphia Daily News*, and the *Washington Post*. Moreover, Vu-Text is building a national network that will include many of the newspapers published by Knight-Ridder, as well as the full text of the Pennsylvania Legislative Database and the *Academic American Encyclopedia.*

In many of these sources, information is available in the online database within 24 hours of publication. While Vu-Text is designed primarily as an information service for the news media and business community, it is indicative of a new trend in communication and electronic information. Future researchers will not search online databases to find references to articles pertinent to their needs, but will retrieve the entire text of materials housed in libraries and computers in any country or town.

Online Encyclopedias

Although the age of electronic delivery of factual, ready reference information has arrived, its value for libraries at this moment is still unclear, and online access to encyclopedias is one example. A small number of computerized versions are available online, for a price. *Encyclopaedia Britannica*, the *Academic American*

Encyclopedia, and the *Kussmaul Encyclopedia* (based on the *Cadillac Modern Encyclopedia*) are offered by various database firms.[4]

In order to decide whether it is worth the cost of going online to search, rather than approaching a subject in the print version, it is essential to consider the differences between print and electronic access and the advantages of each. The typical print version is organized alphabetically by subject, with further access points to subjects provided by cross-references and detailed indexes. The user's manual approach to a query often involves browsing through the entries containing information on a specific subject. In so doing, the searcher is also exposed to illustrative materials that are part of the articles.

Computerized versions seek to justify their cost by allowing unlimited access points for retrieval, which is not universally true, however, now. CompuServe subscribers can access encyclopedias only by assigned subject headings, such as queries to *Academic American* (offered through Dow Jones) or *Kussmaul* (from Delphi). Without the benefits of full-text searching, users are not able to retrieve all entries that contain a desired word or combination of words. Although full-text searching is possible in *Britannica* (via Mead), the vendor is not allowed, at this time, to make this database available to libraries. In addition, no pictures are available online, and much of the beneficial browsing in volumes is eliminated.

Of course, having an encyclopedia online allows more frequent updating than is possible with print versions, and computerized encyclopedias will not be limited to information stored in a predetermined number of volumes. They have the capability to expand readily—even to encompass the type of nonencyclopedic material in other types of reference sources, such as dictionaries and handbooks. At this point, the most dramatic advantage of having an encyclopedia online is its public relations value: calling clients' attention to the fact that access can be provided in a new way. But is it worth what it will cost? The cheapest rate for accessing a pictureless encyclopedia is reported to be $5 per hour.[5]

Hardware

When a microcomputer is available in the school library media center, the basic components of communications between that center and any of the dial-up services are ready. Almost any microcomputer will work: from the small TI/99 to the IBM PC, and including the Apple and TRS-80 machines. In fact, the microcomputer's keyboard and its ability to transform letters and numerals into computer

[4]Gordon Flagg, "Online Encyclopedias: Are They Ready for Libraries? Are Libraries Ready for Them?" *American Libraries* (March 1983): 134.

[5]Patrick R. Dewey, "A Professional Librarian Looks at the Consumer Online Services . . . The Source, CompuServe, Apple Bulletin Board, *et al.*," *Online* (September 1983): 36–41.

code are the essentials of any computer terminal. Other components, necessary for online access, are a

1. Serial communications interface
2. Modem
3. Printer (optional, but highly recommended)

If one plans to store the products of literature searches on floppy disks (a technique known as *downloading*), the following extras are required:

4. A disk drive(s)
5. Communication software
6. Word processing software

A serial communication interface is absolutely essential, but may already be built into the microcomputer. The most common types of serial interfaces have what is known as an RS-232 connector; but this can vary from manufacturer to manufacturer. If a system lacks such an interface, it can usually be purchased for about $150. A *modem* is the device that converts the computer's code into audible signals that can be transmitted over telephone lines (*mo*dulate-*de*modulate). The phrase "going online" is derived, in part, from this process of transmitting computer signals over normally voice-grade telephone lines. Modems for microcomputers can be characterized as internal or external, acoustic or direct connect, and by their data transmission speed.

An internally mounted modem fits into one of the *expansion* slots of the microcomputer; and many internally mounted modems include a serial interface as part of their circuitry. An external modem is a free-standing unit, separate from the microcomputer, which attaches to the serial interface. Acoustic modems require the attachment of a standard telephone headset into a pair of rubber cups after the remote host computer has been dialed up; direct-connect modems attach directly to the telephone lines and allow the user to dial-up through the microcomputer keyboard. Many of the advanced direct-connect modems allow frequently used telephone numbers and log-in procedures to be stored in the modem's memory.

Finally, modems are also characterized by the speed of data transmission they can accommodate. Data transmission is measured by a baud rate (bits per second), and most modems are either 300 or 1200 baud. A 300-baud modem can process approximately 30 characters per second; a 1200-baud modem can process about 120 characters per second. This is important to understand, since baud rate significantly affects cost. The 300-baud modems vary from $100 to $300; 1200-baud modems cost from $300 and up, depending on features. Over the long term, a 1200-baud modem may prove to be more economical, since a search session (usually billed by the hour) can be significantly shorter with a faster modem. Some data vendors, however, charge 1200-baud users more per hour.

If a *hard copy*, a printed record of the online session, is desired, a printer will be required. Printers for microcomputers come in all shapes and sizes. The least expensive ($150 to $300) are thermal printers which print on specially treated roll paper in a dot pattern. Their output is neither attractive nor long lasting. The cost of dot-matrix printers, the most common printers used for microcomputers, ranges from $300 to $1000; they print on plain or fanfold paper in an ink-dot pattern.

Dot-matrix printers definitely have a computer look, but have achieved general acceptability. At the top of the line in computer printers are, of course, the letter-quality or daisywheel machines. The output of one of these printers is virtually indistinguishable from that of the IBM Selectric typewriter. Although their cost is declining, letter-quality printers are expensive ($1,000 to $3,000) and are certainly not necessary for the dial-up services suggested in this chapter.

If one wishes to download data files into machine-readable form, one, and preferably two, disk drives are needed in the system. Floppy disks and disk drives are a *must* for reading programs or storing data. Floppy disk drives cost from $250 to $400, depending on their storage capacity.

To access a remote computer through a microcomputer and modem, a software program is needed. This program is usually loaded from a floppy disk that instructs the microcomputer to emulate the characteristics of a computer terminal. Good communication software, often referred to as *terminal software*, also gives the user the powerful capability of downloading or storing data as a text file onto a disk. Some communication software programs also allow the downloaded data to be set up as a personal database which can be researched. These programs range in cost from $50 to $200.

The most sophisticated communications program, developed by the Institute for Scientific Information (ISI), *Scimate*, combines terminal software, a universal online search module, and a personal data manager. *Scimate* sells for more than $800.

Word Processing Software

Short of using a package like ISI's *Scimate*, a user will need a word processing program to reformat data which has been downloaded and stored as text files. A word processor can make significant cosmetic change in a downloaded data file, creating an attractive client-centered bibliography from raw data.

Training, Initiating Services, and Costs

The school library media specialist will need to understand the basics of electronic information searching, and can gain that knowledge from monographs and journal articles or from formal training programs. Schools of library and information science and some schools of education offer courses. State Departments of Education are beginning to offer training seminars as well. Professional associations also engage in similar activities. And major database vendors offer instruction in various major cities throughout the United States. Although many training sessions require a fee, introductions can be attended at no cost. Potential vendors should be contacted and training needs discussed with them. Although some providers of electronic services believe the manuals they provide are sufficient for inexperienced users without special supplementary training, this is not true for all manuals.

The introduction of dial-up services for students can best be facilitated by working with a small number of individuals, using a limited group of databases. In the simplest approach, the school library media specialist works with one class on a research project which demands information beyond that contained in classroom texts. Use the microcomputer to assist students in their search for bibliographic references online. Select a limited number of online databases for access. This will provide opportunity to perfect your search skills, to learn the advantages of online access, and to demonstrate the direct relationship of the school library media center's services to the curricular needs of students.

One database that should be considered initially is Magazine Index, since it provides coverage of popular magazines that goes beyond the *Reader's Guide to Periodical Literature*, yet is still at a level of sophistication suitable for grades 7 through 12. Many student topics can be searched on this database. (Successful use has been observed for students in classes as diverse as general science and expository English.) Any topic that is suitable for a search in *Reader's Guide* can be attempted on this database. This means that teachers who are responsible for courses in history, science, and English are good candidates for cooperative efforts.

A sample search, typical of the style of research done by high school juniors and seniors, was performed on Magazine Index, via Dialog. The proposed term paper's subject was ''The Holocaust, 1939–1945: Attitudes of the American Jewish Community.'' Magazine Index was chosen for its wide coverage of the popular *and* professional literature, as well as its similarity to the printed index *Reader's Guide*.

Two major concepts were involved in the search: (1) the Jewish Holocaust and (2) American attitudes. The search strategy demonstrates the simple elegance of online searching on a subject that could not be adequately handled manually.

The first task was to build a ''set'' of all documents in the database which contain the term *Holocaust* in their title, abstract, or descriptor fields. The microcomputer retrieved 407 such documents. From these 407, documents that referred to the television miniseries of a few years back were excluded (using the Boolean NOT operator); the remaining documents (or *postings*) in the set numbered 386.

In order to intersect the set of documents which deal with the Holocaust with that set of documents which refer to the United States or things American, a second, extremely large set was constructed, using the Boolean OR operator. This produced 126,510 postings which contained either *United States, America*, or *American* in their title, abstract, or descriptor fields.

The intersection of these sets (using the Boolean AND) left a manageable set of 34 documents which met the search criteria. References were to journal and magazine articles and book reviews, and came from publications as diverse as *Newsweek, Time, Commentary*, and the *Annals of the American Academy of Political and Social Science*. (Articles in *Newsweek, Time*, and *Commentary* would be available to students in their school or public libraries. References to articles in the *Annals of the American Academy of Political and Social Science* would be more difficult to locate.)

The dates of the retrieved articles demonstrate another factor that must be considered in accessing online databases: the extent of their coverage. Of the 34 references produced, 23 were published in the 1980s, 8 were published in the 1970s, and 3 were published in the 1960s. Most online databases originated in the mid-1970s and do not provide retrospective coverage of material. Even a database like Magazine Index, which has made an attempt to index older data, does not extend back past the 1950s. Most printed indexes, on the other hand, go back several decades.

This search strategy, which incorporates many of the features available in an online interaction, took an inexperienced searcher (student), under the guidance of an experienced searcher (teacher), about 15 minutes, at a cost of approximately $3.50. In a pilot program, focused on a senior- or junior-level research project, $3 to $4 per student could be budgeted. It is hoped that such allocations would not come from already existing book and media allocations, but would be new, added budget lines.

Two possible instructional models have to be considered. In the model or example on which this chapter has focused, students are trained to perform their own searches. In the second and more popular model, at the postsecondary level, the search is performed by a trained and experienced professional searcher. Each model has its advantages and disadvantages. The student-as-searcher model provides inexperienced users with a real, hands-on opportunity to test their training and knowledge in the unpredictable world of document access; but it may mean that more time is spent online. Therefore, the cost of searching may be slightly higher. In terms of an instructional approach, the professional-as-searcher model allows students to receive similar training in search strategy and database selection, but adds more control, in terms of time and money, to what actually occurs online. The decision to pursue one approach or the other should be based on the specific goals and objectives established by school library media specialists for their instructional programs.

The big question is, of course, who will pay for access privileges? Will schools create mechanisms that provide students with their own, limited accounts for searching? Or will the rich be the only ones who have access to information on demand? Although this last question is beyond the scope of this discussion, it deserves a great deal of consideration and must be addressed in any discussion of cooperative activities for taxpayers.

Cooperative activities that cross type-of-library lines will undoubtedly include agreements among school, public, and academic libraries that support online activity, including delivery of the documents located online by users in any of these institutions. It may even be possible to consider regional contracts for searching services, i.e., agreements that provide mechanisms to cover costs for students if they wish to do their searching in a location other than the school. The bottom line will be determined by those who create policy.

Interactive Videodisc Technology

Marvin Davis

The videodisc has been defined as "a rigid storage medium for analog or digital data written and read by a laser."[1] The main feature is random access to great quantities of information. At a recent American Library Association conference, one company distributed complimentary 5¼-inch disks holding one million complete MARC records of English-language books. The combination of this technology with the microcomputer permits rapid searching of individual frames of the videodisc.

The term *interactive video* means different things to different people. To some, the term is synonymous with *television*. While the viewer may be physically passive, the viewer's mind is "interacting" with the video and audio in much the same way the mind reacts to real-life events. This is one of the factors that makes television a good teaching aid. An example of interactive video in this sense is people becoming totally enthralled with soap operas and sporting events, or the interactive tension created during a "theatrical" scene of a television play. Many viewers discuss the plots and characters of soap operas or television plays as if friends were involved. However, that is not the definition for this chapter.

For our purpose, *interactive video* will mean the physical interaction of the viewer with the video segment being presented. This definition means that the viewer must touch a portion of the video screen, or enter items on the connecting computer, or manipulate segments manually through the videotape recorder. That is, the viewer must *enter* information, *move* to pre-set segments, *touch* the video screen, or in some way physically interact with the program being viewed.

Interactive video, as defined above, offers an expanded variety of media not now available on the microcomputer alone. However, this combination has not been widely used because of the lack of information about the systems, the cost,

---

[1]"Glossary" (Delran, N.J.: DATAPRO, December 1983).

and the absence of appropriate videodisc programs. This chapter attempts to provide basic information concerning the learning possibilities provided by these systems and a brief analysis of current costs related to development and use.

Cost

As with any technology, the costs are derived from the development and production of hardware and the accompanying software. The current hardware is pulled together from two separate systems, already in place. The cost of a home videodisc system has been greatly reduced since the first machines became available, and the costs of microcomputers are being reduced regularly. However, one must purchase additional hardware to connect these two technologies, because *stand-alone* systems are still too expensive for schools.

Until copyright clearances are fully defined, videodisc software will be produced by companies that own the rights to media which can be placed on a videodisc, or the content must be created for this format. The development costs of software will continue to be greater for videodisc than for microcomputer programs. Producing a film for the videodisc, then accessing this film, will require a greater time investment than writing and debugging the much shorter microcomputer program on floppy disk.

Definition

In defining the interactive video system, one must remember that this medium represents a new technology and should be used creatively, rather than trying to "squeeze" the present instruction media into this format. Interactive video can combine information in books, filmstrips, films, and kits with rapid access through a microcomputer. However, the technology has flaws.

A videodisc is capable of storing over 50,000 frames. While the technology is still not capable of clear representation of letters and numbers (a flaw of the monitor's resolution rather than videodisc technology), it can store color, motion, and sound. The videodisc resembles a long-playing phonograph record in size and shape, but is accessed by laser beam rather than needle or recording heads. The interactive videodisc combines the video storage capabilities of the videodisc with the random access capability of the microcomputer.

The definition of interactive video should carry some suggested uses of this technology. It is an excellent medium in which to show motion, when motion is necessary. It is also an excellent medium when seeing the actual picture, graph, map, or chart is necessary. It can provide students with slow-motion photographs. It is an excellent means to show size relationships. This medium provides all the propaganda possibilities of film and television. Last, it has great storage capacity. One videodisc can store all the paintings in the collection of the National Gallery of Art.

On-Off Sequencing

In its earliest form, the viewer physically started and stopped the video recorder by a command from the video or audio portion of the program. The viewer then recorded responses on paper or performed the designated operation. At the end of the sequence, the viewer restarted the videotape recorder and continued the process.

In other variations, the viewer proceeded in the same manner, but the time allocated for response was part of the videotape. The tape continued to run for a pre-set time while the requested functions were performed. This second method eliminated the need to start or stop the recorder and assured that the process was completed in a pre-set time. A more advanced variation allowed for a pre-set order of various types of selected segments. Different segments, or variations of the same segments, were developed to better meet the learning needs of the individual.

In still another variation, responses were recorded on a separate device which analyzed the answers and either continued with the learning sequence or responded with a review session. One of its main problems was the limited responses which were acceptable as an answer to any question. This forced the program designer to use some form of multiple-choice question. If an ''open'' question was asked, the variety of acceptable or correct answers was greatly reduced. Indeed, the viewer might be stating a correct response which was not programmed into the sequence.

The greatest drawback to these types of interactive programs was that they did not allow for individual differences and paid limited attention to the rate of learning. These methods allowed for slight variation, but each variation was essentially linear in nature, rather than branching. The linear program not only made minimal allowance for individual differences, but reinforcement was virtually nonexistent. The combination of the microcomputer with the videotape player or the videodisc allowed for almost unlimited combinations of segments and graphs, questions and answers. However, the videodisc was definitely superior to the videotape, because access to any segment of the videodisc was instantaneous whereas the videotape required rewind time, whether forward or backward.

Because it was necessary to maintain communication between the processor and the video player, only those players in which the playback head maintained control with the tape during the search mode could be utilized. The videotape contained two channels which were read or played simultaneously (e.g., the head must stay on the tape). Track 1 contained the audio while track 2 held the commands for the videotape recorder.

In general, the microcomputer interacted with the player via the second channel of the audio track. The microcomputer controlled the frame that was to be shown—the delay, review, and so forth—all by the predesignated code on the sound track. The microcomputer then controlled the tape player, provided the graphic or visual, scored the answers, and directed the pattern of learning by branching, based on students' answers. The programs were developed in such a way that wrong answers provided for a remedial sequence or review.

Normally, a program would not allow the viewer to progress to the next section until the correct answer was provided. If reviews were utilized, this meant the simple repetition of the same segment, until the correct answer was selected or made as a response. In more sophisticated programs, the answer that was selected determined the next segment to be seen. The new segment might provide the information in smaller steps or explain why the selected answer was wrong. A sequence of correct answers allowed the viewer to proceed at a faster rate, either by moving to a more advanced level or proceeding through the same level in less detail.

Operating the System

In many programs, viewers control the program and record their answers by means of the microcomputer keyboard. Thus, the viewer must know not only how to operate the video equipment, but also the microcomputer. If the equipment comes in separate parts, then the various connections between the microcomputer and the video player must be made. In most cases, the connection consists of a separate *board,* which must be placed within the microcomputer, and the connection wires are hooked to the video player. In order to use the graphics in most systems, the video portion must be used, and this requires a *monitor* rather than a standard television set.

Many instructional designers feel that the switch from video for viewing to the microcomputer for answering is a distraction and may tend to interfere with learning. Lack of keyboarding skills may also reduce the rate of learning and cause frustration to the viewer. Systems are being developed to overcome this by a touch-sensitive video screen—an infrared grid that indicates to the microcomputer the portion of the video screen that is being touched. Programs which use this technology allow the viewer to remain totally involved with the video screen and relieves them of the need for keyboarding skills.

Touch-sensitive systems are particularly useful for teaching electronics, diagramming, and diagnostic testing and repair. It is the format most used by the military in its training programs. An encyclopedia uses this means to let children choose among topics to research. Given pictures of objects, such as five animals, the student chooses by touching an animal on the screen. This produces a new screen, giving information about that animal. While the touch-screen method can indicate one of several multiple-choice answers, development of this format for testing is too expensive at the present time.

The Current Scene

The early videodiscs were developed only to show what a videodisc is and what it could do, rather than to educate. The cost of producing videodiscs has delayed large-scale development and production of educational programs. The lack of both software and compatible equipment has limited interactive videodisc use by the education community. Many available programs are still in the beginning stages: programs are selected and the learning objective that they might teach is then determined, rather than identifying a learning objective and building the visuals and graphics necessary to teach the objective.

New technologies are lowering costs and improved technologies are providing expanded production in graphics. Already, affordable software systems are beginning to appear. One of these takes the extensive filmstrip library of a major company, puts the filmstrip frames onto a videodisc, and provides the software needed to access any of the desired frames. School library media specialists must plan for the installation of this or a similar system in the future. Training programs for this combination are being tested in both the military and the business community. These test sites serve as guideposts, in much the same way that the military training film demonstrated to teachers the educational use of film in the classroom.

While educators are beginning to recognize the potential benefits of this technology, the industry moves ahead, but slowly. In Currier's words, "educational applications for interactive video have multiplied, and the number of firms offering products or services has more than doubled."[2] Yet the technology is still in the development stage. The school library media specialist can purchase videodiscs of the type now being developed by the Library of Congress and NASA. Inaccessible materials, such as early movies made before sound, as well as photographs taken during NASA projects, are being preserved on videodisc.[3] They could be useful in secondary film classes and science classes and projects.

Training disks for auto mechanics are being developed—programs that use a variety of audiovisual formats with interactive video, including random access slide projects, computer-text graphics, videotape, and random access audio.[4] If, after students are asked to identify the parts of the motor, they do not respond correctly, review slides, with additional graphics, expand identifying features. Transferring such applications to other learning tasks appears to be only a short time away.

---

[2]Richard L. Currier, "Interactive Videodisc Learning Systems: A New Tool for Education Creates Powerful Visual Lessons," *High Technology* 3 (November 1983): 51–59.

[3]Thomas R. Dargan, "Computer Management for a Videodisc Production," *EITV* 15 (June 1983): 37–38.

[4]Murdo Cameron, "An Interactive Training Environment for Pilots," *EITV* 15 (June 1983): 34–36.

School library media specialists should watch for the following phenomena as interactive video appears:

1. Expanded use of the characteristics of the medium, such as separate and distinct audio channels, access to a single picture, and random access to those pictures, with control from the microcomputer
2. Numerous options, such as digitized audio and computer-generated text, and the development of graphic images
3. Meeting the needs of different target audiences with different levels of information on a single disk
4. User control through menus, indexes, remedial and advanced tracks, and individual pacing
5. Modification of videodisc programs[5]

These characteristics of the interactive videodisc will permit the school library media specialist to choose from a wide variety of information provided on a single medium, as well as help teachers modify that information when needed, provide the same information on a variety of learning levels, meet individual student needs quickly, and allow information changes to meet curriculum changes.

Over the next few years, perhaps the most noticeable increase in all forms of interactive video will be the home market, in which newsletters and magazines will not only be available but the readers will be able to interact almost directly with the editor. This, when combined with the current trend toward voice-interactive microcomputers, will make learning (as well as communication) possible without written responses or touching the video screen. At this point, the viewer will interact with the video and microcomputer in whatever language is selected. Not only will it be possible to use the same program in various countries, but that program could teach various languages through direct interaction with the "almost-live" situation. "Readers" of videodiscs will be able to browse through them, in much the same way that readers browse through books. The school library media specialist will help teach this process.

The Future

Interactive video and videodiscs are changing access to all types of information, and may change—even more radically—the methods of presenting information currently in other formats. It is likely that some videodiscs will be produced by reformatting several existing programs on a specific subject. Just as book publishers have asked school library media specialists to recommend subject areas which have not been covered in the literature, suggestions for subject content to be placed on videodiscs could be made by individual school library media specialists.

---

[5]Michael Yampolsky, "The Next Generation of Interactive Videodiscs," *EITV* 15 (June 1983): 44.

Since they are aware of the available materials for specific subject areas, their suggestions should assist a videodisc producer choose from a variety of media presentations on a given subject.

As the production of interactive video systems expands, students will be able to access motion, sound, text, and still pictures from a single source and decide if further research is required. If most of the information collected on a videodisc is too difficult for students, they may be able to exchange one videodisc for another on the same topic, but at an easier reading level or on a more basic concept, just as they have been able to choose a different book or encyclopedia.

It will be possible for the teacher and library media specialist to work together to revise information on a videodisc if it becomes as easy to record on videodisc as on videotape. It will be possible to use a different filmstrip, an additional picture, a new text. At this point, *students* may be able to choose the learning materials to add to the disk. In the Socratic manner, learning will truly become a unique experience, appropriate to its time.

Computer Literacy in Secondary Education

James LaSalle

During the past few years there has been a determined effort to provide secondary school students with some type of computer literacy. However, opinions have differed widely on the content of these courses, which students to include, and what constitutes a computer-literate student. Most definitions of the term *computer literacy* include the history, theory, and operation of personal computing machines, to the extent that individuals have a basic knowledge of the technology and the ability to interact successfully and exert control over it.

The problem is to create a flexible form of computer-literacy education; any plan for a permanent curriculum is impossible. The rapid changes in computer technology and its assimilation into the home and workplace make any course outline subject to obsolescence almost before it has been distributed to students. In addition, the adoption of computer technology in elementary schools will further change (if not cancel) plans for the entire computer-literacy effort at the secondary level.

The course description which follows was created for a junior high school, and the general format of the sample course covers four main sections: (1) history, (2) hardware, (3) programming, and (4) applications. It might be convenient to consider the content as "computers for the masses." Topics in the course must be of interest to the majority of the student population and enable them to function in a computerized world. Students who desire to probe the esoteric workings of computer machinery can be tracked into a rigorous computer science course.

Our outline provides four modules, each of which begins with a brief introduction and is followed by suggested topical outlines. The time frame is a one-semester course, taught daily for one class period.

Module 1: Computer History

Computer history is omitted from some computer-literacy courses, and this makes it difficult for students to appreciate the complexity of today's microchip technology. Microcomputers, which many take for granted, had their beginnings with two pre-silicon titans, Mauchly and Eckert. Even the vacuum tube hardware of the 1950s is indebted to the simple devices of Babbage, Jacquard, Pascal, and the unknown inventor of the abacus. It is important that students view the computer as a device in development, as today's advances lay the foundation for tomorrow's breakthroughs.

Studying computer history not only helps to foster respect for the sciences, but paves the way for discussions of computer hardware. Instead of simply memorizing hardware terms, students will understand how and why a particular item was named (e.g., "So *that's* why that key is marked RETURN.").

In this 45-hour computer-literacy course outline, sufficient time should be allowed for library media center research on key historical figures, and computer history should be allotted a minimum of 8 school days.

It is important that the student be able to define a computing device, and this pristine definition will suffice for junior high school: *A computer is a device that can (1) perform calculations and (2) store and follow instructions.* Class discussions can track the evolution of counting mechanisms to computing machines by testing this definition against the devices listed below. This approach can simulate the binary decision-making process of digital computers.

    I. Computer History
        A. Early Counting Devices
            1. Fingers, stones, marks
            2. Abacus
            3. *La Pascaline*
        B. Transition Machines
            1. Jacquard's programmable loom
            2. Babbage's analytical engine
            3. Hollerith's census tabulating machine
            4. IBM's Mark I
        C. Computing Devices
            1. First Generation (Vacuum Devices)
                a. Large physical dimensions
                b. Large use of electricity
                c. Unreliable
                d. Topics to develop: ENIAC, EDVAC, EDSAC, John von Neumann, UNIVAC

2. Second Generation (Transistor Devices)
    a. Size and power consumption decrease
    b. More reliable
    c. Costs decrease
3. Third Generation (Integrated Circuits)
    a. Further decrease in size, power consumption, and operating costs
4. Fourth Generation (Large-Scale Integration)
    a. Greater component density
    b. Microprocessor
5. Fifth Generation (Very-Large-Scale Integration)
    a. Computer on a chip

Module 2: Computer Hardware (Theory)

The study of computer hardware is very interesting to junior high school students if they have access to the very equipment being discussed in class. Besides, they are eager to learn how the computer device they may have received as a gift operates. This is one of the most enjoyable segments of a computer-literacy course. The dialog between students and teacher is stimulating for all involved.

Much teacher preparation is required to keep abreast of ever-changing hardware innovations; however, the interest exhibited by students makes the extra research worthwhile. First-time computer-literacy teachers can use the traditional subsystem approach (input/output, central processing unit, mass storage) to introduce such topics as time sharing, word processing, and common databases. (The latter encompasses computer crime and the horror stories of a computer running amok among ''magnetic'' money records, causing great hardships to hundreds of hapless humans. Temper these stories with the fact that computer hardware is incapable of making arbitrary decisions. Computing hardware is only an *extension of a programmer;* and although the electronic Frankenstein is a popular topic, it has been overdone.) A suggested computer hardware outline follows.

II. Computer Hardware
    A. Central Processing Unit
        1. Microprocessing Unit
            a. Arithmetic/logic unit
            b. Control function
        2. Clock
        3. RAM and ROM Memory
    B. Input/Output (I/O) Unit
    C. Mass Storage
        1. Paper Media (Punched Cards and Tapes)

2. Magnetic Media
   a. Tape (digital tape construction, proper care and handling, recording techniques)
   b. Floppy disk (construction, care and handling, recording techniques)
   c. Hard disk (construction, care and handling, recording techniques)

Module 3: Computer Programming

The widespread acceptance of BASIC as a computer language makes it the best choice as a vehicle to sample programming for the junior high student. Although the teacher may prefer Pascal (which is used on the SAT advanced placement test for high school students), FORTRAN, or COBOL, remember that this is a *survey* course. Computer literacy is *not* an introduction to a programming course. BASIC is "resident" on too many personal computers to ignore. And if students are expected to perform any assignments at home, the instructor must use the language of the most popular computers. At this writing, it is BASIC.

This segment of computer programming requires meticulous attention to detail. Ownership of a BASIC-speaking computer does not automatically qualify an individual to teach programming. One only has to read a newsstand-variety computer magazine to find evidence to support this position. John Nevison's book on programming style is required reading; it is highly recommended for both the novice and experienced programming instructor.[1]

Many BASIC programs, as often published in magazines, are a hash of whatever code was necessary to accomplish a given task. Little structuring is evident and no attempt is made to make the programs readable. Many editorials cite BASIC as the cause of this sorry state. It is true that some languages lend themselves to top-down structuring techniques more easily than others (Modula 2, Pascal, C, and others), but it is wrong to fault BASIC as the primary cause of tangled logic. The bottom line is good programming, and problem-solving techniques are possible in most present-day programming languages.

Program generation may be summarized in four broad steps:

1. Define the problem.
2. Create an algorithm.
3. Translate to a computer language.
4. Debug (remove errors).

Good programming begins with thorough definition of the problem at hand, before its transformation to a high-level computer language. Inasmuch as the in-

---

[1]John M. Nevison, *The Little Book of BASIC Style* (Reading, Mass.: Addison-Wesley, 1978).

tent of a computer-literacy course is to provide a familiarity with computers, the instructor must assume responsibility for the definition phase of program creation. This allows students to concentrate on creating a working algorithm and its subsequent translation into BASIC. The emphasis is on the computer as a problem-solving tool, rather than a puzzle in itself.

Algorithms may be expressed in several popular notations; however, the flowchart is a common symbolic representation. (See figure 1.) Another method of graphically representing a sequential series of actions is the Massi-Shneiderman flowblock. (See figure 2.) Finally, the simplicity of pseudocode should not be overlooked.

Figure 1. A sample flowchart

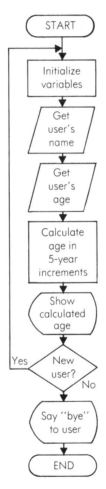

Figure 2. A sample flowblock

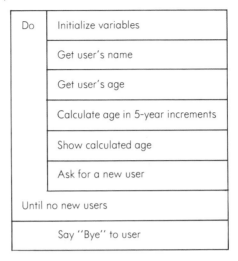

Pseudocode is a synthesis of English and a computer language. No special templates or artistic skills are necessary to utilize this format. The following example demonstrates the use of pseudocode in developing a simple BASIC program.

Problem Definition. Write a computer program that asks one or more computer users for their names and ages. Each person's age (in 5-year increments) is calculated and displayed. Now the computer asks if the program should be repeated. If the answer is negative, the computer says "good-bye" to the user.

Algorithm in Pseudocode (First Pass).

    Program name: NameAge
    Repeat
        Initialize variables
        Get user's name
        Get user's age
        Calculate age in five years
        Display calculated age
        Ask for another pass
    Until there are no new users
    Say good-bye to user
    End of program

This pseudocode could be easily translated into Pascal, COBOL, FORTRAN, Modula 2, or virtually any computer language. One might say pseudocode, or its pictorial equivalents (Nassi-Shneiderman diagrams, flowcharting), is a truly portable computer language. Each "pseudostep" is expanded until a program emerges; that is, the coding of the final product into a specific computer language is independent of planning the program sequence. The stylized TRS-80 (Microsoft) Level II BASIC program (figure 3) is the result of repeated "polishing" of the proposed pseudocode. Each instructor should develop a classroom "standard" program form. This will provide direction for the students and facilitate the correction of programming assignments.

Figure 3. A sample Level II BASIC program

```
10 REM Filename: NameAge.Bas
20 REM Updated: 04/25/84
30 REM by J. LaSalle
40 REM
50 REM Program Description
60 REM      A styled demonstration program that determines
70 REM the computer user's name, current age, and his/her
80 REM age five years from today.
90 REM
100 REM      Variables Dictionary
110 REM      — — — —
120 REM QUery$      Holds user's response to query
130 REM ALias$      User's name
140 REM AGe         User's age
150 REM
160 REM
400 REM ******* Begin Main Program *******
410 CLS                          :REM Clear screen
420      LET ALias$ = " "
430      LET AGe = 0
440      LET QUery$ = " "
450 REM
460      INPUT "What's your name"; ALias$
470      INPUT "How old are you"; AGe
480      PRINT
490      PRINT ALias$; "will be"; AGe + 5 ; "years old in five years."
500      PRINT
510      INPUT "Do you want to do another"; QUery$
520      LET QUery$ = LEFT$(QUery$,1):REM Check Y or N as 1st charact
530      IF QUery$ = "Y" THEN GOTO 410        :REM Repeat loop
540 PRINT "GOOD-BYE"; ALias$
550 END
```

Contrast the program in figure 3 with the sample program shown below—the BASIC "stew" that is typical of programs published in newsstand-variety computer magazines. Which program would you rather debug or explain?

```
1 CLS:A$ = " ":A = 0:Q$ = " ":INPUT"WHAT'S YOUR NAME";A$:INPUT"
HOW OLD ARE YOU";A:PRINT:PRINTA$;" WILL BE";A+5;" YEARS
OLD IN FIVE YEARS.":PRINT:INPUT"DO YOU WANT TO DO ANOTH
ER";Q$:Q$ = LEFT$(Q$,1):IFQ$ = "Y"THEN 1 ELSE PRINT"GOOD-BYE "
;A$
```

These programs are simple, with no error-trapping input routines; the point is, however, it's easier to learn programming from the first listing than from the compressed code.

Given the 45-day restrictions on this computer-literacy course, only a BASIC "sampler" of commands may be covered. Using Microsoft BASIC as an example, include the following commands or instructions in your BASIC vocabulary.

LET	PRINT	RUN	LIST	NEW
REM	IF. .THEN	GOTO	INPUT	TAB
END				

Looping structures should be developed with IF. .THEN/GOTO combinations. If time permits, the FOR. .NEXT loop may be introduced; however, it may be prudent to defer this command for a more advanced course.

Programming emphasis in a computer-literacy course should be on the structure and sequential logic of the program. The skills developed should be those which can be successfully transferred to programming other computer languages. Some programming practices detract from the readability and logic of the program, and should be avoided. Indeed, care should be taken to discourage development of such habits.

Examples of *non*constructive programming in BASIC follow:

1. More than 3 commands in a multiline statement
2. Absence of REMark statements
3. More than one END statement
4. No END statement
5. Excessive use of GOTO statements
6. Transfer of program control to a REMark statement
7. No variable dictionary in the form of REMark statements
8. Repetitive code, instead of subroutines
9. No attempt to "pretty" loop structures
10. Complete absence of spaces between key words
11. No attempt to use meaningful variable names
12. No clear exit routine from program
13. Absence of error-trapping routines

Module 4: Computer Applications

The final module of the course can be the most creative. The objective is to help students understand how computers affect their lives and how to exert some control over this phenomenon. General topics which might be included are as follows.

IV. Computer Applications
- **A.** Personal Computing Applications
  - **1.** Word Processing
  - **2.** Information Storage and Retrieval
  - **3.** Text Reviews
- **B.** Computers in the Home
  - **1.** Appliances
  - **2.** Communications
  - **3.** Entertainment
- **C.** Computers in Everyday Life
  - **1.** Banking
  - **2.** Shopping
  - **3.** Recreation
- **D.** Computers in Government
  - **1.** Records
  - **2.** Taxes
  - **3.** Crime
- **E.** Current Issues in Computing
  - **1.** Privacy
  - **2.** Copyright
  - **3.** Crime
- **F.** Control of Computers
  - **1.** Malfunctions
  - **2.** Accuracy Checks
- **G.** Computers as a Career
  - **1.** Communications
  - **2.** Engineering
  - **3.** Art
  - **4.** Telecommunications

Any of the four modules can include field trips, guest speakers, demonstrations, simulations, debates, research, and other activities designed to explore the present and the future of computers in society.

Our sample computer-literacy outline for junior high students is an overview rather than a computer science course. Its objective is to inform and to provide enough "coverage" to interest the general student while providing the first step for students who wish to pursue continuing interests. While flexible in most respects, it presupposes a knowledge of programming. Library media specialists who have learned to program may wish to teach it. For the purpose of completing classroom assignments, the essential elements can be merged into appropriate courses.

PART FOUR

WORKING WITH
THE FACULTY

With software and hardware in place and services planned, the ongoing challenge of working with the faculty begins. Having provided teachers with materials, the media specialist now becomes responsible for their proper use. One of the most diverse opportunities faced by the library media specialist is to work with teachers to assist them in learning how to use the hardware and in integrating the use of the microcomputer into the curriculum. The school library media specialist is responsible for assisting teachers in knowing the capabilities of the microcomputer, from both an educational and an operational point of view.

A first step in this process is to understand the possibilities offered by the microcomputer programs which offer computer-assisted instruction. Part 4 begins with an article on computer-assisted instruction. The second article proposes a taxonomy of microcomputer use. The next article describes inservice and continuing education opportunities, the most obvious area in which the library media specialist will work with faculty. This part ends with specific uses of the microcomputer in subject areas.

Review of Research on Computer-assisted Instruction

David V. Loertscher

One of the greatest contributions that a library media specialist can make in the microcomputer revolution is to help with the curricular uses made of this technology. Those who advocate the use of microcomputers in education often do so on the basis of dreams for the technology rather than of a proven track record as revealed in research. It would seem wise, therefore to: (1) know what can be expected from the theoretical viewpoint, (2) track what happens in schools as experiments are conducted with the technology, and (3) keep abreast of research findings.

The purpose of this section is to summarize what is known from research about computer-assisted instruction and what these results mean to the school library media specialist. Happily, there are a number of analyses and reviews of research already in the literature, and this body of literature is likely to grow very rapidly in the next few years. The meta-analysis technique, developed by Gene Glass at the University of Colorado, combines the findings of many experimental studies. The reviewer takes the results of data analyses reported in the summary statistical table, the F table, of each experimental study and combines the experimental variance across studies. For this chapter, meta-analyses were organized by educational level—elementary, secondary, college, and adult findings.

Since there are a number of terms dealing with the use of computers in learning, a single term will be used for convenience, computer-assisted instruction (CAI). The acronym will be used for such terms as computer-assisted learning, computer-managed instruction, computer-directed learning, and others.

Research Relating to Elementary Schools

In 1982, Vinsonhaler and Bass reported their summary of thirty experimental

---

[1]J. Vinsonhaler and R. Bass, "A Summary of Ten Major Studies of C.A.I. Drill and Practice," *Educational Technology* 22 (December 1982): 29–32.

comparisons in ten schools.[1] They concluded that CAI drill and practice were more effective than traditional instruction in raising standardized test scores.

Electronic Learning Laboratory at Columbia University reported in 1982 that student attention, defined as time-on-task, was higher with computers than it was in the classroom.[2] This conclusion is not surprising because the computer usually requires the student to interact constantly with it during an instructional program. It can even be programmed to measure the number of responses per minute made by the students and the number of incorrect or spurious responses to questions. In this way, the teacher can get some measurement of time-on-task for the student in a given lesson.

Ragosta and Jamison evaluated drill and practice curriculum of the Los Angeles schools for Educational Testing Service (ETS) in 1981.[3] Their findings indicated that CAI has a positive impact on computational math, but that it does not necessarily increase conceptual understanding. Language and reading results were not as positive as those in math. Gains were the greatest in the middle elementary grades.

Hartley, in his meta-analysis of CAI done in 1977, found that CAI was one of the most effective ways of teaching mathematics in the elementary school.[4] The reader should note that 1977 predates the emergence of the microcomputer. His review, therefore, is of large, main-frame applications.

Two other pre-microcomputer reviews were found, one by Edwards et al.[5] and the other by Jamison et al.[6] Both found CAI to be an effective teaching tool, particularly for students who were below grade level.

Elementary and Secondary School Studies

Three reviews were found which spanned both elementary and secondary schools. Henry Becker, at Johns Hopkins University, has written a review and concept paper on computers and has published the results of a national survey of the uses of microcomputers in schools. In his later survey, the preliminary report shows that, at the elementary level,

micros are largely employed as cost effective means of increasing the rate at which students learn the rules of arithmetic computation and proper English usage. Secondary

[2]Electronic Learning Laboratory, *On Task Behavior of Students During Computer Instruction vs. Classroom Instruction* (New York: Teachers College, Columbia Univ., January 1982).
[3]Marjorie Paul Holland Ragosta and Dean Jamison, *Computer-Assisted Instruction and Compensatory Education: The ETS/LAUSD Study. Final Report* (Princeton, N.J.: Educational Testing Service, 1981).
[4]S. S. Hartley, "Meta-analysis of the Effects of Individually Paced Instruction in Mathematics" (Ph.D. dissertation, University of Colorado, 1977).
[5]Judith Edwards *et al.* "How Effective Is CAI? A Review of the Research," *Educational Leadership* 33 (November 1975): 147–53.
[6]Dean Jamison, Patrick Suppes, and Stuart Wells, "The Effectiveness of Alternative Instructional Media: A Survey," *Review of Educational Research* 44 (Winter 1974): 1–67.

schools, which have more microcomputers than elementary schools, tend to use their micros to teach students about computers and to teach them how to program in BASIC. So do elementary schools that have had computers for two or three years. There is a decline in the use of micros for drill and practice as programming teaching increases. Many teachers reported that the main impact microcomputers have had is social. More enthusiasm for schooling, a greater tendency for students to work without a teacher, and more instances of students helping each other were among the trends mentioned. As previous studies have shown, lower income public school districts are much less likely to have school microcomputers.[7]

In another review published in 1981, Burns and Bozeman warn that, while CAI has been shown to be effective in teaching math, there are a host of variables to consider and control if positive results are to be expected.[8]

Clement, in his review for *Educational Technology* in 1981, concentrated on the affective results of using CAI.[9] He found that, in general, student attitudes toward computer-based education have been positive. Some of the reasons given are:

1. self-paced instruction (there is time to absorb and comprehend the materials without inconveniencing another person)
2. lack of embarrassment when mistakes are made (only the computer knows)
3. immediate feedback (immediate knowledge that the answer is correct or incorrect
4. a general feeling that the student learns better through the computer system
5. lack of subjective evaluations, i.e., the computer bases its evaluations strictly on student performance, not on personal characteristics or on the social relationship with the teacher.

Secondary School Studies

Two reviews of research were located which dealt with only secondary students' use of CAI. Kulik, who does very careful and quality controlled syntheses, performed two meta-analyses of CAI studies, one on the secondary level and the other on the college/adult level.[10] In the secondary school review, his analysis of 52 ex-

---

[7]Henry Jay Becker, "School Use of Microcomputers" (Baltimore, Md.: Center for Social Organization of Schools, Johns Hopkins Univ., April, June, October, 1983; February 1984).

[8]Patricia Knight Burns and William C. Bozeman, "Computer-Assisted Instruction and Mathematics Achievement: Is There a Relationship?" *Educational Technology* 21 (October 1981): 32–39.

[9]Frank J. Clement, "Affective Considerations in Computer-Based Education," *Educational Technology* 21 (April 1981): 28–32.

[10]James Kulik *et al.* "Effects of Computer Based Teaching on Secondary School Students," *Journal of Educational Psychology* 75 (February 1983): 19–26; "Synthesis of Research on Computer-Based Instruction," *Educational Leadership* 41 (September 1983): 19–21.

perimental studies showed that students receiving CAI scored at the 63rd percentile on tests, compared to the 50th percentile for the "no CAI" group. CAI improved retention and also the speed at which students learn; this was true across various subject matter areas. However, his analysis covered only drill and practice.

Thomas, in his "pre-micro" review in 1979, affirms the power of computers as teaching tools and suggests that many students receiving CAI gain mastery in a shortened period of time.[11]

Summary of All Studies

As a summary of all the research completed to date, the following conclusions are supported:

1. Most of the research thus far has concentrated on drill and practice and much of the research has been done with large main-frame computers.
2. Most studies agree that CAI is an effective teaching tool and possibly a little bit better than conventional instruction.
3. Positive affective results can be expected as children and young people interact with computers.
4. Better time-on-task behavior can be expected.
5. Significant time savings can be anticipated when using CAI.

Those are the positive findings. In addition, there is a trend away from drill and practice applications in math and language arts. This finding is interesting since almost all research has been done for those applications. It means that, as school library media specialists move away from drill and practice applications, they are doing so without a large body of research to guide them. Becker notes that the trend is toward the teaching of programming. So far, there is little research which shows the effect of programming skill on other educational skills.

In looking at the research on CAI, it is easy to get a feeling of *déjà vu*. Every technology in education has been shown to affect learning positively; that is, children and young people learn, no matter what method is employed. That conclusion should not be surprising to any school library media specialist. At first, technology has been held up as a dynamic tool that might revolutionize education, and then it has faded into obscurity as time has passed. The reasons for disappointment with technology are legion; however, failure is not usually due to the technology itself but, rather, to the ability to use it.

---

[11]David B. Thomas, "The Effectiveness of Computer-Assisted Instruction [in] Secondary Schools," *AEDS Journal* 12 (Spring 1979): 103–15.

Misuse of Technology

Disappointment with microcomputers has already begun to surface:

A significant number of schools that have computers are not using them very effectively, if at all. Some computers sit on the shelf, and some teachers that originally had
high expectations about the difference computers would make now feel misled or disillusioned. The reasons for this situation vary. Some schools bought expensive hardware
only to discover that it isn't what they really need and doesn't do what they thought it
would. Some schools have computers, but no money at all for software. Some have
computers and software, but no staff members with the information, guidance, and the
experience necessary to use them and to work with students effectively. And so many
schools that have a computer, some software, and some experience are still asking
themselves in frustration, "What difference can a single computer possibly make to so
many children?"[12]

In addition to the criticism of unplanned and chaotic microcomputer use in
some schools, other scholars are worried about a new generation of inequality
based on "haves" and "have nots." Others are worried that the division between
the sexes will grow wider in what is perceived to be a male-dominated computer
culture. It should be pointed out that negative feelings toward technology in education may be rampant from time to time, but it is no more severe than criticism of
teachers and their methods. Three considerations merit our attention when considering the effectiveness of technology:

1. A technology should not be expected to deliver more than it was designed
   to deliver.
2. If technology is to deliver, the potential must be used wisely.
3. Poor materials and programs created for the technology must be rejected,
   and only tested and proven software must be selected.

Sadly, many teachers lack training in the use of any educational technology.
Too often the teacher passes the subtle hint to students, "Sit back and relax while
this film entertains you" or "I've taught you what's really important. Technology
will now provide supplemental or enriching experiences." Teachers should require as much or more attention while students use technology as when they are
experiencing any other form of instruction.

One instructional event which should *not* be chosen for microcomputers in
schools was described by Becker.[13] In his study a single microcomputer was put in
each of six classrooms. Teachers were given a short inservice training program
and were encouraged to use the computer any way they wished. No courseware
for the computer was provided, and so most teachers tried to teach a little pro-

---

[12]Jean Varven, "The Schoolhouse Apple," *Softtalk* 3 (June 1983): 123–24.
[13]Becker, "School Use of Microcomputers."

gramming. The computer was available to the students for three weeks and the research staff made on-site observations and followup interviews. Each student had an average of ten minutes of microcomputer time over the three-week period. While teachers were generally grateful that they had had the experience, Becker was disillusioned about what a single microcomputer could do in a classroom.

The question to be asked is, "If you give a child ten minutes to work at a microcomputer, what can you expect to happen?" Obviously the answer is, "Nothing." Why criticize a technology and its promises if it is used so thoughtlessly? It is ludicrous to attempt a computer literacy curriculum with a *single* microcomputer in each school. A single microcomputer can make a difference, but only when careful planning and wise utilization will allow it to do so.

If microcomputers are to be used successfully in schools, school library media specialists should be the leaders in their use in schools. Who else in the school has more experience with technology than the staff in the school library media center?

If the research can be believed, microcomputers will have a lasting role in education. Their role in schools for the management of instruction and in library media centers is already assured, and better programs and ideas for their use in teaching are emerging so rapidly that it is extremely difficult to keep current.

What the school library media specialist can do is to exploit microcomputers, to use all of their capabilities as valuable teaching tools. Leiblum lists the characteristics of microcomputers that should be exploited.[14] He says to choose instructional events for microcomputers which:

1. Telescope time and images (compress them into a short period of time).
2. Provide an active response by the student. (The student should be pressing keys and inputting responses every few seconds.)
3. Use the power of the microcomputer to generate problems or data. (The microcomputer can draw graphs, present math problems, and calculate results.)
4. Provide multiple presentation levels for individual students. (The microcomputer analyzes the level of the current user and matches teaching to that level.)
5. Provide information storage and retrieval. (Microcomputers can store bibliographies which can be searched by any key word.)
6. Provide real-time experiences. (Microcomputers can create actual drawings or models based on data entered and constraints given.)

For the learner, he suggests that programs be chosen which will:

1. Provide active response and feedback. (Students actively interact and know whether they are progressing.)

---

[14]M. D. Leiblum, "Factors Sometimes Overlooked and Underestimated in the Selection and Success of CAI as an Instructional Medium," *AEDS Journal* 16 (Fall-Winter 1982): 67–79.

2. Provide learner control. (The microcomputer allows students some choice over content, speed, and direction.)
3. Be self-pacing (allow the student to indicate when a screen will change).
4. Be scheduled at the convenience of the student. (The program and equipment are available at any time.)
5. Be repeated at any time the student needs it. (The microcomputer program allows the students who need more practice than others to have the practice without penalty.)

The uses of microcomputers in the curriculum are just beginning to be explored by school library media specialists. Whether this medium delivers all it can deliver will not be decided in the research arena, but in the software industry and at the individual school level. If this technology repeats the past pattern, it will be a useful tool to a few teachers, a baby sitter for others, and ignored by a sizeable segment. As the first excitement dies down, the impact will be in direct proportion to its wise use, and library media specialists have always been able to encourage and expand the appropriate use of media. What school library media specialists have learned from the research is that microcomputer technology has delivered to educators a finely made shovel. Two things can be done with the shovel. One can lean on it or take hold of it and dig.

Computer Coordinator Involvement in Instruction

David V. Loertscher

The role of the library media center in relation to the use of microcomputers is affected by the title of the person who coordinates the program. Be this person the library media specialist or a computer specialist who is part of the library media staff, the following are stages in the computer coordinator's development.

1. Microcomputer center warehouse—Facilities, equipment, software, and documentation are available for students and teachers.
2. Individual consultation—Students and teachers receive information about microcomputers and software.
3. Informal planning—Attempts to encourage teachers and students in microcomputer involvement usually take place in the hall, teacher's lounge, or lunchroom. ("Here's an idea for an activity and new materials to use. Have you seen . . . ?")
4. Evangelistic outreach—A concerted effort is made to promote the integration of microcomputers into the curriculum.
5. Scheduled planning in the support role—Formal planning is done with teachers or students to supply software or activities in response to a previously proposed unit or project.
6. Instructional design—The computer coordinator participates in every step of the development, execution, and evaluation of an instructional unit which has a computer component.
7. Curriculum development—Along with other educators, the computer coordinator contributes to the planning and integration of microcomputers into courses of instruction.

An adaptation of David V. Loertscher's taxonomy appeared in "The Second Revolution: A Taxonomy for the 1980's," *Wilson Library Bulletin* 56 (February 1982): 415–16.

The foregoing shows steps for the library media specialist or computer coordinator, which start with passive services and go to active services. Ideally, the person filling the role would provide a mix of all the levels rather than providing service at one level to the exclusion of others. It is not enough for a person concerned with providing and supervising a microcomputer laboratory to serve only a technical role rather than a professional one.

Working to provide services requires an in-depth approach to working with faculty. The following step-by-step plan is proposed as a pattern. It assumes that a computer coordinator is capable and can communicate with the faculty as a true colleague in instruction.

The Teacher and the Computer Coordinator
A Planning Process[1]

Step One: The teacher and the computer coordinator plan together.

A. During a first meeting, identify what unit of instruction is to be planned and the approximate dates to be taught.

B. When necessary, briefly discuss the abilities and interests of the students.

C. Determine the objectives of the unit:
1. Clarify and simplify the objectives.
2. Are the objectives manageable in view of the microcomputer resources of the school?
3. Bloom's taxonomy considerations:
   a. Knowledge
   b. Comprehension
   c. Application
   d. Analysis
   e. Synthesis
   f. Evaluation.
4. Discuss microcomputer characteristics which could contribute to the unit.

D. Decide what each person is expected to do before the next meeting.

Step Two: The teacher and the computer coordinator prepare.

A. The teacher and the computer coordinator locate hardware and software remembering:
1. Levels of difficulty
2. Interest levels
3. A variety of microcomputer software types (drill,

---

[1] Adapted from the work of Marilyn Goodrich, Beverly White, and David V. Loertscher by David V. Loertscher and the IMPAC Computer Class, University of Arkansas, Summer 1985.

simulation, problem solving, tutorials, applications and others)
4. Software for special students
5. Software and hardware from other sources outside the school
6. People resources.
B. Prepare creative ideas:
1. Ideas for microcomputer activities involving commercial programs or locally produced programs
2. Ideas for effective use of microcomputer software
3. Ideas from the school's computer literacy continuum
4. Ideas for building logic skills, thinking skills, problem solving skills, and evaluation of microcomputer software.
C. Meet again:
1. Discuss unit content changes, if necessary.
2. Discuss microcomputer software available and preview, if necessary.
3. Discuss creative ideas.
4. Decide exactly who will be responsible for presenting each microcomputer activity in the unit.
D. Prepare and test, if necessary, the software and activities.

Step Three: The teacher and the computer coordinator present the unit.

A. Jointly introduce the unit and its objectives and activities.
B. Carry out planned activities. Be open to change as the activities develop.
C. Share enthusiasm with students.
D. Expect students to achieve the objectives.

Step Four: The teacher and the computer coordinator evaluate.

A. Together, evaluate:
1. Unit objectives and content.
2. Materials and equipment:
   a. Enough?
   b. Interest and difficulty suitable?
   c. Variety of software sufficient?
   d. Was program user friendly?
3. Activities:
   a. Motivated?
   b. Lead to unit objectives?
   c. Worth the effort and cost?

B. Seek input from students on any of the above topics.
C. Test learning (cognitive, affective, and psychomotor):
  1. Paper and pencil tests
  2. Computer tests
  3. Other types of tests (including learning from computerized materials, not just lectures and texts)
  4. Tests from any computer literacy continuum skills.
D. Followup:
  1. Plan to teach the unit again?
  2. Materials or equipment need replacing?
  3. New software or hardware need to be ordered?
  4. Any issues which should be submitted to administrators?
  5. Successes and failures reported to appropriate administrators?
  6. Any other plans to make?

Library media specialists will recognize the four-step process as instructional design. This process is applicable to all media available in the school or district. Every professional working in the library media center should be comfortable with the role of instructional developer. This role extends beyond the creation of a microcomputer warehouse and concentrates on making the seemingly heavy investment in this new technology pay off in terms of increased learning of students. Students deserve quality experiences with microcomputers. Working with the teacher can ensure them.

Training Staff and Teachers in the Use of Microcomputers

E. Blanche Woolls

Use of high technology requires continuing education and training for many educators. These are new and very exciting opportunities for the school library media specialist: to learn the technology and to teach it to others. Learning about high technology is the same type of challenge which confronted earlier librarians when they were introduced to a new labor-saving device, the typewriter. At that time, articles were written not only about the potential usefulness of this typing machine, but also about the harmful physical effects which could be inflicted upon persons who typed all day. Potential physical harms are described in relation to new technologies today, and these anticipated detrimental effects are one of many of the excuses which may be used by persons who are resistant to new technologies or change. It is a factor which must be recognized by library media specialists.

Tackling a wide variety of new technologies is not a new experience for many library media specialists. Resistance to new types of equipment (video cameras and recorders) or more advanced models of existing technologies (automatic filmstrip/tape players) was overcome in the 1960s when large quantities of media were produced for educational use in a wide variety of formats. Selection of the best for the library media center collection continued to be the responsibility of school library media specialists who learned to judge the quality of media in relation to criteria beyond those applied to book selection (e.g., since motion is necessary, a film is appropriate). These persons then helped their teachers make careful choices before expending funds. Included with the additional responsibilities of choosing software and assisting teachers with selection came the necessity of choosing the best hardware. Selection of software and hardware for any new technology, including the use of high technology such as the computer, remains the responsibility of the library media specialist.

Pioneers in Library Media Center Computing

The degree of implementation and the quality of use of high technology offered in the school library media center are dependent upon many factors, but the most critical is the expertise of the staff of media centers. For those who wished to adopt mainframe computer technology in the early 1960s, a lack of suitable programs and access was a serious hindrance. Mainframes were housed in district headquarters. Where mainframe computer access did exist, it was under the direction of business managers. These persons and their data processing staffs did not readily welcome school library applications because they seemed low on the district's priority list, as contrasted to a high-priority use such as school district payrolls or scheduling classes each semester, or even scoring district-wide standardized examinations. However, a small number of school library media specialists were able to convince top administrators of the need to develop mainframe applications for library media management.

School library media specialists in the Albuquerque, New Mexico, schools, in the Leavenworth, Kansas, High School, and in the Shawnee Mission, Kansas, schools implemented and then reported their use of mainframe computers in the early 1960s. Mainframe computer use at the school level was largely due to these pioneers. Widespread acceptance of this form of technology failed to occur because of the cost of computers, as well as the low priority of school library functions on the district computer processing cycle. Microcomputers eliminated these handicaps, but the same problem, associated with innovation, remains.

Many school library media specialists had no programming training or experience, and few opportunities were available for them to learn outside of formal classes. At the present time, interested school library media specialists are choosing a wide variety of methods to secure the needed training. A few recent graduates have had courses in computer languages and computer applications, and some have had microcomputer-use classes. Others are finding that newer microcomputer programs are so "user friendly" that an extensive training period is not needed to use microcomputers in their centers.

Attitudes have adjusted to the belief that microcomputers are just another piece of equipment. Learning to use any tool which is to be used by teachers and students, or which will save time and energy in media center management, is a high priority for most school library media specialists today.

Teaching Computer Literacy to Staff and Teachers

No established body of knowledge exists to build from basic knowledge to "computer literacy." No standardized methods are proposed to step from a lack of knowledge to competence, although standardized tests have been developed. In fact, as stated earlier in this book, a wide variety of definitions exist for what "computer literacy" really means. The method chosen for learning about microcomputers depends upon the definition of "computer literacy" and the level of expertise desired.

Computer novices often do not understand what they need to know about microcomputers. Many persons do not realize what level they have attained, based upon the training they have received, and will not know if they need to continue at a very basic level or have gained skills which make it appropriate for them to enter an advanced workshop. They may not be able to judge if the proposed curriculum will meet their needs.

While many persons who are developing a training curriculum for introducing others to the microcomputer teach programming (and only programming) in these beginning sessions, it is the premise of this author that one can be computer literate with very little knowledge of programming. The microcomputer program user need not know how to program, any more than the user of a 16mm film in the classroom needs to be able to produce a 16mm film. Another illustration might be the person who uses a pattern to cut out and sew a dress or to construct a doghouse. Many people prefer to use someone else's design rather than create their own. Still others choose only the ready-made product. The designer of the original pattern for the dress or the doghouse is similar to the programmer who tries out the various pieces to see that the pattern works. Some persons like to take this pattern and choose their own applications, or different fabrics or materials, while others prefer the choice of finished products.

Somewhere between the two opposite poles is choosing to create all microcomputer programs which will be used in the library media center, or using only those programs which have been created by others—that very wide area with persons who want to learn a little about programming so they can better understand the theory of computing and the mechanisms for making the computer function. It is true that one does not need to be a mechanic to drive a car, but it helps to know where the engine is and how to add gasoline to the tank. With the microcomputer, one must choose which programming language to learn and how deep to explore.

Training Opportunities Outside the Local School or District

Professional association members at the local, state, and national levels, recognizing the need for training, organize lectures, workshops, and laboratories at association meetings. In Florida the state association, the Florida Association of Media Educators (FAME), works very closely with the state department of education to plan and offer a series of microcomputer workshops throughout the state. Certainly the American Association of School Librarians conferences since 1982 have provided a number of opportunities for school library media specialists to begin or continue their experiences with microcomputers.

Some state departments' personnel offer microcomputer workshops throughout the area. The first of these usually acquaints participants with the potential of the microcomputer. As an example of this, early in 1980 Gary Neights, with the Pennsylvania Department of Education, began organizing and presenting Microcomputer Administrator Demonstration Days throughout the commonwealth. School administrators and media personnel were invited to attend these one-day regional demonstrations. One-week workshops were then scheduled to expand training for intermediate media staff who were encouraged to replicate the training throughout their intermediate area. Following this, one-week sessions were (and are being) presented to school library personnel.

Entire departments of universities and colleges are offering computer science, and other university faculty have planned noncredit continuing education experiences for teachers and school library media specialists. Teachers-in-training are offered microcomputer options as a part of their coursework or their student-teaching-methods experience. In some institutions, units have been added to existing courses or full-credit courses are offered in microcomputers in education. Most university credit courses are applicable to advanced degrees and for salary increment steps.

In many locations, vendors have established laboratories and offered free training to anyone who is willing to attend classes. School personnel, opting for this training, attend classes with others who are not necessarily school teachers. Participants receive basic instruction and information concerning programming languages and the software available for their machines.

Planning Inservice Programs

Whether one is training school library media center staff or assisting teachers in using high technology, a number of considerations must be given to planning the inservice programs. The first of these is the general criteria for inservice training which have been adapted for microcomputer applications.

1. Define "computer literacy" as it will be implemented in the school district.
2. Inservice training programs must be planned to meet the needs of the teachers, administrators, and staff for which they are intended. To accomplish this, a needs assessment should be made of the teachers—anonymously, for most are reluctant to admit they know very little. In many cases, some carefully defined choices should be indicated so that persons with no awareness of what they need to know can have help in choosing from what is available.
3. Novice teachers should assist in the planning to assure that needs are addressed. Nothing is as insulting as to attend an inservice program whose

leader assumes the audience has no training or knowledge about the subject being presented. If the persons being trained participate in the planning, they will readily indicate if a part of the program is too elementary or too advanced.

4. Needs are established, based upon the status of the microcomputer program in the school district. Is this program at the beginning stages, slightly more advanced, or is it in place and expanding?
5. Inservice training programs must allow participants to operate the demonstrated equipment. Necessary resources, and expertise, must be available to provide adequate experiences. For teaching microcomputer use, no more than two persons should be assigned to one microcomputer.
6. Appropriate measures should be taken to assure that all participants receive similar training.
7. An outline of what is to be covered should be established to make sure that people "begin where they are" and progress as far as they can go, in the time allocated.

Once the definition of computer literacy has been determined, needs have been assessed, participants have discussed the proposed program, and plans have been finalized, the inservice can be implemented. An example of one training program is presented below.

A Model Inservice Program

This training module is designed from one used in carrying out a funded microcomputer training project for teachers and library media specialists in one region of a state. This project is offered as a model to be adapted for use elsewhere.

Basic needs are identified through meetings with administrators, teachers, and school library media specialists in the surrounding area. This includes a single school, a school district or a consortium of public school districts, parochial schools, and private schools. The needs statement includes the following:

1. Computer literacy training for school districts exceeded the school's ability to train teachers except in brief training sessions.
2. Professionals with the skills necessary to offer instruction were too expensive for most school districts.
3. Free vendor training appeared to be hardware-centered and did not provide tools for evaluating alternative products.
4. The rapid introduction of new technology typically produces resistance to change, and this resistance was recognized.
5. Teachers need help to overcome resistance to microcomputers as technology advances for classrooms.

Furthermore,

6. Teachers and school library media specialists need different levels of computer literacy training, ranging from basic selection and operating skills through systems evaluation to instructional program development.
7. Teachers and school library media specialists need advanced computer-literacy training for administrative and research applications, curriculum development, online search and communications, and networking operations.
8. A need exists for training trainers to transfer computer literacy directly to their individual schools.

Training is offered on four levels. The first level is designed to provide basic computer literacy. A 45-hour program, made up of 14 units, teaches terminology and vocabulary and allows introductory hands-on use and practice in systems operation.

Six units cover the use of common software packages. Skills (and practice) in storing, protecting, and retrieving software files; tools for assessing and specifying the educational and operating requirements that new software packages or user-developed programs should meet; and simple programming procedures are discussed. A programming project permits practice in writing a simple program. Tools for comparing and evaluating software alternatives and procedures for assuring that software packages meet performance requirements are stressed. Package maintenance and software package storage, security, backup, and onsite upgrading are presented.

Finally, special-purpose packages for writing instructional programs are demonstrated, and curriculum opportunities for using microcomputer programs are identified. Introductory textbooks to achieve computer literacy are assessed for their completeness and use within an individual school.

Level 2 (24 hours of instruction) is the intermediate computing literacy program, and participants continue the development of their programming skills. Professional methods for modifying programs are shown, and classroom issues for educators introducing computer literacy for students are stressed. An in-depth treatment of professional techniques for modifying existing program systems is a part of this level.

Another 24 hours of instruction are given during level 3, which is designed specifically for school library media specialists, although interested teachers may attend the sessions. This program stresses the choice of software for administrative and management applications for school library media centers. Tools for assessing student skills, as well as assessing attitudes toward microcomputers, are discussed. Library media specialists are provided with evaluation techniques to judge the needs of their schools. Online professional database searching is taught and the potential of the microcomputer is demonstrated. Accessing the OCLC database and the use of the microcomputer to download this data, interlibrary loan procedures, and electronic mail applications are shown. (A much longer description of training for database searching and the possibilities with electronic mail are given earlier in this book.)

Level 4 (also a 24-hour module) is designed to train trainers to transfer the above curriculum to schools. A group-centered training program was developed in collaboration with the trainees themselves and with representatives from the schools involved in the inservice training program. Teaching aids and practice in microcomputer demonstration were stressed.

What Comes after Literacy?

In many school districts, regional systems, and entire states, major efforts were made to provide computer literacy for teachers in the early 1980s. But, as the newness of any technology wears off, efforts to promote use, offer inservice training, or provide funding for software and hardware are forgotten. To say, "We had a three-week microcomputer inservice course and all our teachers are now trained," is no more accurate than it is with any other educational technology. The technology changes; software changes; research findings are published. Teachers must be updated on a regular basis if the technology is to be exploited.

Two case studies of computer literacy efforts illustrate this problem. In one school district, a math teacher who knew more than others about computers was selected to do an extensive inservice training program for the faculty. Month-long inservice sessions on operating and programming the microcomputer were planned on a rotating basis. In a two-year cycle, 80 percent of the teachers had been through the training.

The school district supplied every school with fifteen to twenty microcomputers. In the elementary schools, the microcomputers were placed in the library media centers. In the junior high and senior high, the microcomputers were placed in computer laboratories. Computer literacy classes for students and computer science classes filled the microcomputer laboratories, leaving no time for any teacher to use the microcomputers for subject area applications. Only in the elementary schools was there any opportunity to use the laboratory for something other than programming. The superintendent of the district bragged that all his teachers were computer literate.

In the second district, inservice was planned by the library media specialist and a group of interested teachers. Microcomputer use was stressed and word processing programs and curriculum integration were demonstrated. Teachers were recognized for their use of microcomputers for classroom projects. The superintendent of this district also bragged that most of his teachers and students and all of his library media specialists were computer literate.

In reality, the initial excitement of any new technology will not be sustained when teachers discover they neither have access to the technology nor have access to adequate collections of software. Purchase of equipment without planning brings the entire concept of microcomputers and computing into question.

Whether library media specialists accept a leading role in educational computing in their school or district, they have the responsibility to understand this role. They also must have the competence to demonstrate the improvements microcomputers can make in instruction, and they should be familiar with enough types of software and software packages to assist all teachers in using the microcomputer in the classroom. If library media specialists can demonstrate competency in the use of this technology, teachers will accept their leadership.

Efforts at inservice training for computer literacy will fail if follow-up is not planned and monitored carefully. The experience gained with experimentation in classes and library media centers should be documented so that it can be the basis for retraining sessions for teachers by grade level or by subject or just small groups of interested teachers.

The library media specialist who teaches an innovation such as word processing or database searching will contribute to the writing process in all subject areas. Inservice training can be organized around a single topic, word processing, for example. Word processing can integrate writing throughout the entire curriculum, not just in creative writing classes. This ''thematic'' approach to training is likely to have greater impact than a general overview session which many teachers may have already had.

Summary

A wide variety of training programs and computer-literacy courses are described in the literature and may be adapted or modified to meet needs. However, the library media specialist must consider the amount of information which can be given in the limited time available for most teachers. Programs must be planned which will aid their teaching or management practices. This may not be easy, for some teachers may still feel inadequate in comparison to their more computer-wise colleagues and students. Some excellent beginning, user-friendly, and easy-success programs could help overcome initial reluctance. All teachers should become interested in word processing programs, skill-building programs, and administrative programs such as grade books. If the trainer starts with these, it will help move teachers into more sophisticated applications at a later time, if this is considered a necessary step.

Do not anticipate immediate conversion of all teachers. (The only educationalevent acceptable to all teachers is summer vacation.) Many will continue to resist change and new technology. If they perceive that they are forced to use microcomputers, they may sabotage the program. Certainly the excitement of students will help provide the incentives to get most teachers to plan for the use of microcomputers in classrooms or to send their students to the library media center to use microcomputer programs.

Expect some teachers to misuse the microcomputer. (Misuse of other forms of media, such as the Friday afternoon movie, is not a new phenomenon.) It is futile to try to stop this behavior, and it will take much effort to modify it. Examples of good student and teacher use of microcomputers, presented by teachers during teachers' meetings, may help to reverse contrary attitudes.

Library media specialists realize that computer technology is ever changing. Hardware, software, and applications are constantly invented, improved, and expanded. The library media specialist must be constantly on the alert for new-equipment demonstrations, new products to share with teachers, and all training opportunities for students, faculty, and staff. Methods to acquire the new skills essential to the teacher and the library media specialist, who live in an era of high technology, must be brought to the attention of all.

Developing a District Plan for a Middle-sized School District

Jean Donham

The Iowa City Community School District serves over 3,000 K–12 students in 15 elementary and 4 secondary schools. Within the district, both curriculum and advisory committees devise strategy for developing curricula; and an additional advisory committee was established to develop a framework for the use of microcomputers in classroom instruction. The committee was composed of elementary and secondary school principals and teachers, one elementary and one secondary school library media specialist, and two central-office administrators; the chairperson was the district library media coordinator. Because the committee met during school time, substitutes were hired for teachers and library media specialists so they could serve on the committee.

In this district, leadership in the instructional use of microcomputers has come largely from the library media specialists at the building level. The library media coordinator has demonstrated considerable initiative in the planning for curricular areas at the district level. In addition, the library media specialists from across the district have become knowledgeable about this new technology and its potential for education. The interest of all media specialists in learning about these new resources has positioned them for involvement in computer-assisted instruction.

Development of the district's plan for instructional uses of microcomputers involved seven major steps:

1. Research
2. Development of a philosophy
3. Establishment of a scope and sequence of computer applications
4. Teacher inservice
5. Selection and allocation of hardware
6. Selection of software
7. Evaluation

Research

There is no reason to ''start from scratch'' in developing a plan for microcomputer use. Instead, a planning committee should review what other districts have done, glean from them the ideas that are successful and appropriate to the local situation, and avoid those things which appear to have been mistakes. The microcomputer advisory committee used three types of information sources for research: outside consultants, periodical literature, and conferences.

Every school district can identify, in its local area, human resources knowledgeable about computers. Those resources may come from the Extension Service of a land grant university serving the area, from the local business community, from a nearby college or university, or from a neighboring school district. In Iowa City, because the resource most readily available was the University of Iowa, the committee invited three speakers from the university, each representing a different perspective on computers in education: Kathryn Alesandrini, whose area of expertise is computer-assisted instruction; William Bozeman, from educational administration; and James Johnson, from the university's computer center. The diversity of background, perspective, and opinion was important. It prompted the advisory committee to evaluate each point of view in relation to perceptions of the students' needs and the school district's limitations in money and personnel. The committee met with each speaker separately and asked them general questions:

1. How would you describe the current direction of microcomputer applications in education?
2. Where do computer literacy, programming instruction, and computer-assisted instruction fit into a district's overall plan?
3. How do you recommend a school district allocate its limited resources (money and staff) to respond to the demand for microcomputers in the schools?
4. What inservice (i.e., content) is necessary for classroom teachers who plan to use microcomputers?

Current educational literature is replete with articles about the uses of microcomputers in instruction, and the committee reviewed a number of publications.

Various members of the committee attended conferences relevant to the use of microcomputers in instruction. Often, the reports from these conferences included case studies from other school districts.

The information from all these sources was then discussed by the committee. Comparisons were made between different points of view, and consideration was given to the Iowa City district's characteristics in size of schools, staffing patterns, current curriculum, and inservice structure.

Philosophy

Two kinds of synthesizing resulted from this discussion: (1) an outline of instructional computer applications which appeared appropriate for the district and (2) a statement of philosophy for instructional computing in the district. Instructional computer applications were classified into two categories: teaching *with* and teaching *about* computers.

Teaching *with* computers:

1. Computer-assisted instruction (CAI) is a system in which a student interacts with a computer. The computer is used to provide instruction in the form of drill and practice, tutorial, or simulation. The materials used in CAI are selected by the teacher to complement the classroom curriculum and to meet the instructional needs of the student.
2. Word processing is a system which allows students to compose on the computer keyboard and "save" their work, so that it can be recalled, edited, and printed out.

Teaching *about* computers:

1. Computer awareness is familiarity with the computer's physical characteristics, its uses in daily life, and its operation. It is an initial step toward computer literacy.
2. Computer literacy is knowledge of how computers are used, how computers are programmed, the components of the computer system, and how computers create change in society.
3. Data management is knowledge of commercial data-management systems for organizing the storage and retrieval of information. Familiar examples include VisiCalc and DB Master.
4. Programming is the process of giving directions to the computer by using a language system compatible with the equipment. It involves learning a logic system and a glossary of commands and statements.

After the committee reviewed all the information gathered from consultants, literature, and conferences, a statement of the accepted information was developed to provide a guiding philosophy for the district. The recommendations of this committee were based on several tenets:

1. Computer education is needed by the current generation of students.
2. The computer is both a subject of study and a medium for instruction.
3. Curricula related to computers must provide for a wide range of differences in the learning needs and interests of the students.

4. Computer literacy is comprised of four "hows":

    a. How computers are used as tools in many kinds of tasks

    b. How people direct computers to perform desired tasks

    c. How computer systems work

    d. How computers create change in society.

5. Interaction with a computer is an essential experience for all students at some time between grades K and 12.

In recognition of these tenets, the Iowa City Community School District will provide its students with educational experiences which will acquaint them with the nature of computers and the roles of computers in our society.

Scope of Computer Applications

The applications identified as appropriate by the committee were studied and taught at corresponding levels in the district. In "placing" these applications, four concerns were considered: teacher knowledge at various levels, availability of software, current curriculum, and cost.

At the elementary level, three aspects were identified as priorities:

1. *Computer awareness.* A unit was developed to be taught to upper elementary students by the library media specialist. (Topics include the historical development of the computer, components of a computer system, application of computer technology in daily life, and basic operation of the computer.)

2. *Computer-assisted instruction.* Software was (and is) selected at the district level; then teachers identify the "approved" software appropriate to their students' needs.

3. *Word processing.* Upper-elementary-level teachers may opt to introduce students to word processing as a part of the language arts curriculum.

(In addition, computer programming instruction is available to students at the elementary level through the district's Extended Learning Program [in Saturday classes] and Enrichment Summer School, both of which are tuition-supported programs.)

At the secondary level, inasmuch as computer literacy was identified as a need for all students, a unit was developed to be taught to all students as a part of the required eighth-grade typing course. It extends the awareness units of the elementary level. Topics include components of a computer system, problem solving with a computer, impact of computers on society, computer logic, computer ethics, and how computers are programmed. This is not a course in computer programming; however, students are taught that *people* control computers by giving directions to these machines.

An additional priority for the secondary schools is a sequence of electives in programming: two courses in BASIC, one in Apple-machine language, and one in Pascal. Also at the secondary level, word processing and data management were identified as skills to be taught in business education and to be used in teaching writing in English courses. Finally, some use of district-approved software in computer-assisted instruction was identified as an appropriate application throughout the curriculum.

Teacher Inservice Training

Four immediate needs for classroom teachers' inservice training were identified:

1. Operation of the microcomputer
2. Integration of CAI materials into the curriculum
3. Software evaluation (especially for curriculum coordinators and library media specialists)
4. Word processing (especially for language arts teachers)

Inservice programs in these four areas have been developed and offered at both the district level and the building level.

Selection and Allocation of Hardware

The advisory committee reviewed the ways in which microcomputers would be used in the district. The available hardware was evaluated on the basis of how well each make and model would meet district priorities. Such criteria as cost, availability of software, availability of local service, expandability, keyboard, and memory were considered. However, greater importance was placed on the availability of software and the keyboard design, since priorities at both levels included computer-assisted instruction and word processing. Consistency across the district was discussed, and the committee opted for one model to facilitate across-district sharing of inservice and software.

Because a greater number of applications was recommended for secondary schools, most of their equipment was purchased first. (Schoolwide, the ratio of microcomputers to students is 1:40 at the junior high level and 1:70 at the senior high.) Microcomputers are shared among the 15 elementary schools in sets of 5 computers for six to eight weeks at a time. (During that time, the computers are used in the upper elementary level at a ratio that ranges from 1:18 to 1:25, depending on school size.) In addition, each elementary building owns at least one computer. Future plans call for additional purchases for elementary schools, so that computers will be available throughout the school year in adequate numbers to accommodate demand.

Selection of Software

A district-level software committee evaluates instructional software, using procedures developed by MicroSoft and available from the Department of Computer and Information Science at the University of Oregon. The Software Selection Committee is composed of elementary and secondary library media specialists and teachers and is chaired by the library media coordinator. No software is purchased unless its company or vendor will allow previewing. Approved software is listed quarterly and the lists are distributed to all schools. The District Media Center owns a copy of each approved title, so that schools can preview titles before purchase. Each school then purchases software which is appropriate for its population and curriculum. Library media specialists are key decision makers on software selection at the building level.

Evaluation

The framework for using computers in instruction is under constant review. The committee has resisted pressures for excessively long-range planning and, instead, has opted for flexibility and continuous review. Input is sought from building-level staff through written evaluations and informal discussions. In a time of rapidly changing technology, such flexibility is essential.

Summary

Careful planning is essential as a school district begins to use microcomputers in instruction—especially because the mass media have stimulated great pressure on schools to move into instructional computing. Personnel in each district must assess the potential uses of microcomputers for instruction, the characteristics and needs of the schools and staff, and the cost-benefit ratio of computing activities. Only then is a district ready to commit large sums of money to computers. The technology will not go away, and so educators must plan carefully for effective use.

The seven steps involved in developing this district's framework are all essential to that planning process. The library media specialists of a district, who bring expertise and experience to that process, must take the initiative to be involved in the planning for effective instructional use of this technology.

Language Arts, Reading, and English

Judith B. Palmer

In the early stages of its technology, many language arts teachers dismissed the microcomputer because it appeared that subjects such as mathematics and science would be the only ones with enough applications to be benefited. Recent developments, however, indicate that they are reassessing their position. Software developers have made new efforts in this area, and professional associations are giving major attention to the use of microcomputers for improving language arts.

Much attention has been, and continues to be, given to microcomputers in the literature. A number of literature and research reviews are available and should be read as they appear. One example is *Word Processors and the Writing Process: An Annotated Bibliography*, which covers the literature through 1983.[1] Another example is "Horses, Carts, and Computers in Reading: A Review of Research."[2] An important source is the National Council of Teachers of English which issues many publications about microcomputers, one of which is its "Guidelines for Review and Evaluation of English Language Arts Software."[3]

The use of microcomputers in language arts is determined by three types of software available: interactive courseware that is used for skill building in reading, communicating, and grammar; courseware that is used to help the student develop as a creative writer; and word processing software.

---

[1]Paula Redd Nancarrow, Donald Ross, and Lillian Bridwell, *Word Processors and the Writing Process: An Annotated Bibliography* (Westport, Conn.: Greenwood, 1984).

[2]David E. Tanner, "Horses, Carts, and Computers in Reading: A Review of Research," *Computers in Reading and Language Arts* (Summer/Fall, 1984): 35–38.

[3]National Council of Teachers of English, Committee on Instructional Technology, "Guidelines for Review and Evaluation of English Language Arts Software" (Urbana, Ill.: NCTE, 1982).

Programs to Build Skills

The microcomputer (and available software) can provide either individualized instruction for each student in a class or remediation or extra practice where the greatest need exists, depending on the time, equipment, and software available. This can be achieved through the use of tutorial programs that provide instruction and have the capability to "branch" the students to the suitable part of the program, based on their answers. These programs provide instruction, drill, tests, and progress reporting. This type of courseware is available for reading comprehension, spelling, grammar, punctuation, and other communication/language arts skills. Vocabulary and other programs are designed specifically to prepare students for their SATs. Many of these programs can be modified by the user, a feature classroom teachers will find valuable as they become more familiar with the uses of the microcomputer. Some examples of this type would include "Diascriptive Reading,"[4] which is a full reading program, and "Microspeedread,"[5] which uses print materials and disks to build reading speed and comprehension.

Computer-assisted library instruction programs are useful in helping students learn about specific reference materials, such as magazine indexes, *Current Biography, Bartlett's Familiar Quotations*, almanacs, and the card catalog. One interesting program is "Where in the World Is Carmen Sandiego?"[6] which involves a search for a thief around the world. Clues are given but require use of *The World Almanac* to solve. The advantage of these programs is that they teach the student to locate and use library media center materials as they are needed, build their competency for research and writing, and provide built-in motivation. It must be understood that the time it takes the average student or teacher to achieve the computer literacy necessary to use most of the skill-building software can be measured in minutes, not hours.

An important aspect of the skill-building program is that it allows the microcomputer to interact with each student. It can refer to the student by name, provide immediate feedback regarding answers, and supply immediate reward. These programs usually have branching capabilities that enable them to re-teach, provide reinforcement, or test in response to a student's work. The student's scores can be kept on the disk and unlocked for review by the teacher. Programs should be accompanied by "documentation" that includes the instructional goals and objectives, as well as all information and guidance for student and teacher to use the programs as they were designed to be used.

Programs often include materials that can be used by the teacher to provide

---

[4]Carol Buchter and Ron Buchter, "Diascriptive Reading." Apple. (Freeport, N.Y.: Educational Activities, 1985).

[5]"Microspeed." Apple, IBM. (Greenwich, Conn.: CBS Software, 1984).

[6]Dane Bigham, "Where in the World Is Carmen Sandiego?" Apple. (San Rafael, Calif.: Broderbund, 1985).

pencil-and-paper reinforcement, along with the microcomputer exercise. It is important that teachers have objectives in mind as they examine descriptions of software programs, and later as they use these programs, before they consider them for final approval and purchase.

Programs written in a game format, utilizing inviting color graphics, are also available to help develop skills in reading and the language arts. Programs with titles such as "M-ss-ng L-nks,"[7] which is a reading game to develop use of context clues, "Reader Rabbit,"[8] in which prereading skills are taught in a colorful, musical multiple game format, and "Word Spinner,"[9] which is a decoding skills drill and game, are just a few in a growing group.

Reviewers of educational software should keep curriculum content and goals in mind as they select programs. Students should be directed to meaningful activities that are in line with the school's educational program. This software should be available in the school library media center so that students can use it on their own or as directed by the language arts teacher.

Programs to Help Develop Writing Skills

Excellent software to help children and young people develop their writing skills is available. These programs may be described as "pre-word processors" or "writing assist" software. "Story Machine,"[10] "Kid-Writer,"[11] "Story Tree,"[12] and "Bank Street Story Book"[13] are just a few titles that help students get ideas for writing and provide them with word processing assistance. These programs even offer graphic illustrations for students to include in their creative writing.

Some programs help students organize their thoughts before turning to a word processor to write the story or the research paper. Examples of this type are "Thinktank,"[14] and two MECC programs, "Writing a Narrative" and "Writing a Character Sketch."[15] Another program, "Compupoem,"[16] assists students in writing poetry.

---

[7]"M-ss-ng L-nks." Apple, Atari, Commodore, IBM. (Pleasantville, N.Y.: Sunburst, 1984).

[8]"Reader Rabbit." Apple, Commodore, IBM. (Portola Valley, Calif.: The Learning Company, 1984).

[9]"Word Spinner." Apple, Atari, Commodore, IBM. (Portola Valley, Calif.: The Learning Company, 1984).

[10]"Story Machine." Apple, Atari, Commodore, IBM. (Cambridge, Mass.: Spinnaker, 1983).

[11]"Kid Writer." Apple, Commodore. (Cambridge, Mass.: Spinnaker, 1983).

[12]"Story Tree." Apple. (New York, N.Y.: Scholastic, 1984).

[13]"Bank Street Story Book." Apple, IBM, Commodore. (Northbrook, Ill.: Mindscape, 1984).

[14]"Thinktank." Apple, IBM, Macintosh. (Palo Alto, Calif.: Living Videotext, 1983).

[15]"Writing a Narrative" and "Writing a Character Sketch." Apple. (Minneapolis, Minn.: MECC, 1983).

[16]"Compupoem." Apple. (Santa Barbara, Calif.: South Coast Writing Project, 1980).

Word Processing

One use of the microcomputer, of special interest to all teachers of English and language arts, as well as other curriculum areas which require papers, is word processing. To turn the microcomputer into a word processor, a minimum of 64K of memory, one or more disk drives, a video monitor, and a word processing software package are needed. It is not necessary that *every* microcomputer used for word processing have a printer, as long as one microprinter is available to print out documents. It is nice to have the capability of displaying 80 columns on the monitor, but this is not a necessity. Many microcomputers provide only a 40-column display, and the word processing software is still very effective as a writing tool. The difference is that with the 40-column display, the user cannot see the script, written on the screen, in the format that it will take when printed.

Word processing software enables users to create, change, and print text. One can write reports, papers, poems, letters, lists, memos, and anything else on a word processor. The author can revise and still keep the original. Material can be saved on a disk, updated, and printed as needed.

Skill in using word processing software is valuable for the student writer. Revising is one of the important reasons why this technology is used in the language arts classroom. Teachers report that students do more revising, and do it better, when they use word processors than when they use pencil and paper.[17] The student can rewrite, edit, correct, or just rearrange, without having to write or type the entire text over again. When students use the traditional method of editing or correcting, most of their time is spent on recopying or revising.

The word processor, or word processing software, removes some of the physical difficulty associated with hand writing and can therefore encourage the student to write. It allows students' writing to reflect their verbal ability. The microcomputer itself provides built-in motivation. Research writing is greatly improved by the use of word processing programs, because information can be rearranged easily and quickly. Bibliographies can be enlarged, without changing everything, and footnotes can be added with ease.

Word processing packages are available for all microcomputers with 64K memory. Moreover, this software is available at several levels of sophistication and price. As with other software, the teacher should know whom software is for, and how it will be used, before beginning to examine the descriptive information.

One popular program that is advertised for home and student use is the Bank Street Writer,[18] published by Scholastic. This program was designed to be used by elementary students at the Bank Street School, but is also adequate for personal writing by adults. It allows users to modify the program to work with a particular

---

[17]Brian D. Monahan, ''Computing and Revision.'' *English Journal* 71 (November 1982): 93–94.
[18]''Bank Street Writer.'' Apple. (New York: Scholastic, 1982).

microcomputer. The documentation is clear and very "user friendly," and the disks have a tutorial (on the reverse side) that provides an introduction to the program for students, parents, and teachers. This program is reasonably priced and is often all that is needed for student use. (A more sophisticated program might be beneficial for administrative tasks and advanced students.) One disadvantage of Bank Street Writer is that it can only hold a document 1,300 to 3,000 words long, depending upon whether the computer has 48K or 64K memory. An improved version is available for 128K machines.

Spelling programs that are compatible with word processing programs are also available. One program, Sensible Speller,[19] contains an 80,000-word dictionary and will locate misspelled words and correct them, individually or throughout the text. If the microcomputer finds a word that is *not* in its dictionary, it will display the word on the screen and give the user the opportunity to verify or ignore it. If a microcomputer has two disk drives, 10,000 words can be added to this program. "Sensible Speller" works with a number of word processing packages, but matched spellers are also available. Bank Street Writer has its own spelling package as well as a matched database manager.

Some students will be able to teach themselves, and each other, the ins and outs of the word processing software, once it has been introduced and other students will need extra assistance in getting started. Typing skills are an asset, but not a must. Students can acquire skill and speed at the keyboard with a little practice. Consideration should be given to introducing keyboarding to the very young student.

Several typing programs are available to help children of all ages develop typing/keyboarding skills. One typing tutorial, Typing Tutor II,[20] gives the student a combination of lessons, practice paragraphs, and tests to teach the keys and also allows the teacher to monitor the progress of up to 50 students. MasterType[21] is a similar program with a game approach to increasing typing speed. Whole courses in keyboarding are now available from Southwestern Publishing. These programs are regularly revised and redesigned to improve their teaching of keyboarding and to monitor progress.

Scheduling sufficient time to use a limited number of microcomputers with word processing software might present a logistics problem to the teacher who requires every student to do the same work at the same time. It is much easier if one group uses the microcomputers to write while another group is examining, revising, and correcting a printout of what it has already written.

Almost every student should have this write and then rewrite experience. It has been demonstrated to be beneficial to students with limited ability as well as average and above-average learners.

---

[19]"Sensible Speller." Apple. (New York: Scholastic, 1984).
[20]"Typing Tutor." Apple. (Bellevue, Wash.: MicroSoft, 1981).
[21]"Mastertype." Apple, Atari, Commodore, IBM. (Tarrytown, N.Y.: Scarborough, 1981).

Library Media Specialists' Responsibility

It is the responsibility of the library media specialist to encourage teachers in English, language arts, and reading to take the time to explore the microcomputer and the software market. Word processing is the *single* best application for the language arts area. Its potential is realized most fully when use begins as soon as a child enters school. More than one microcomputer in each classroom is needed, but, from all indications, they are well worth the investment.

Music and Art Applications

Thomas Rudolph

The application of a microcomputer to the music and art programs is one of the most exciting areas for this new technology. While the school library media specialist is willing to help these teachers, it is probable that the specialized equipment needs will predict the placement of some microcomputer equipment in the music and art departments. In elementary schools with no special room for the art and music teacher, one microcomputer in the library should be configured and dedicated to music or art applications. In departmentalized schools, these teachers will need both the use of dedicated microcomputers in their areas and access to the laboratory. The uses described in the following sections have implications for dedicated microcomputers within the departments.

Music

The microcomputer can be used extensively in music education. Current applications of microcomputers and music can be broken into several categories: music theory, music composition, gamelike format, and music performance. These applications can be described as programs designed to develop certain skills or abilities, and they require some background knowledge in the subject area. Music programs are most often designed to supplement a music theory course or to be used in independent study.

Music Theory. At the present time, the Apple computer has the largest number of programs for music and music education. The Apple programs can be put into two categories:

1. Programs requiring an additional music synthesizer board
2. Programs able to run on the Apple without additional hardware or synthesizer boards

Music synthesizer boards enhance the Apple and allow for more advanced production of sound. These boards are quite expensive and must be added to each computer.

The Apple comes with a speaker and is capable of producing single notes. Some software has been written using the Apple speaker. One very good program is Apple Music Theory, from the Minnesota Educational Computing Consortium (MECC).[1] This program, a complete music theory curriculum on one disk, which costs less than $50, is excellent for junior and senior high level. The programs, in the drill-and-practice format, include Name the Note, Wrong Note, Rhythm Play, Musical Terms, and more. Some problems exist with this program as the sound is played through the Apple speaker and could prove annoying if other users are close. Overall, this is an excellent piece of software and highly recommended.

Another excellent music theory program is entitled Practical Music Theory.[2] This series is by Sandy Feldstein and is geared toward beginning and intermediate instrumental music students. These programs are to be used with a music theory workbook, which is supplied with each diskette. They are excellent materials to reinforce music theory concepts in young instrumentalists. Practical Music Theory could also be used successfully in the music theory class and as a class supplement for individual instrumental instruction.

Other programs, which do not use a synthesizer board, are distributed by Wenger,[3] which offers several music theory and music-related programs in the University of Akron series. Brochures and descriptions of these programs can be obtained by contacting Musitronic. The overall quality of these programs is average; however, some of the game-format programs work quite well. As with all computer software, it is recommended that programs be previewed before purchasing.

The best music theory programs are available from Temporal Acuity Products.[4] Its Micro Music series offers a wide variety of software. Most of these programs require the Micro Music (MMI) synthesizer board, referred to as the digital-to-analog converter (DAC) board. The MMI DAC board must be purchased for each Apple computer in order to run the software. The Music Theory programs are extremely well written and can be used at the secondary and college level.

MMI offers programs to drill intervals, chord quality, four-part chord dictation, rhythmic dictation, musical terms, Italian musical terms, and much more.

---

[1] Apple Music Theory. Apple. St. Paul, Minn.: MECC, 1982.
[2] Practical Music Theory. Apple, Commodore. Alfred Publishing Co., 1981.
[3] Wenger Corporation, 555 Park Dr., Owatonna, MN 55060.
[4] Temporal Acuity Products, 300 120th Ave. NE, Bldg. 1, S200, Bellevue, WA 98005 (800-426-2673).

However, it becomes expensive to use the MMI products, as most programs range from $100 to $150—although prices have been dropping in recent months. The overall rating of the MMI series is excellent and a welcome asset to any music collection. Students enjoy while they learn using these programs.

A final vendor worth noting is Electronic Courseware Systems.[5] It offers a variety of music theory software, which should be previewed by music teachers interested in computers.

Music Composition. The second area of programs could be referred to as computer-assisted composition. Most music editors act much like a text editor or word processor. That is, the microcomputer can assist in the composition of music just as it assists in typing a letter. Again, these composition programs can be divided into those that use an additional synthesizer board and those that are able to run through the Apple speaker.

One of the more popular composition programs is from Insoft and called Electric Duet.[6] It allows for two-part composition without the need for additional hardware. The disk costs less than $50 and is useful for the music hobbyist or home user. Although its intonation is totally unacceptable for the music classroom, the program is well written and could be useful if budgets are tight.

In order to compose in more than two parts and with more acceptable intonation, a music synthesizer board must be added to the Apple microcomputer. Several options are available:

1. Micro Music (Temporal Acuity Products) has an excellent Music Composer series which allows for the composition of up to four voices. The notes are entered via the microcomputer keyboard in octave notation. The program displays the music as it is played, but the composer is not able to make a printout of the composition. The "editor" is merely for playback. Added features include programs to develop envelopes and envelope shapes.
2. The ALF Music Synthesizer, from ALF Products Inc.,[7] offers the option of a nine- or three-voice board. The three-voice board is the better of the two and much more in tune. The three-voice cards can be used in pairs to allow for the composition of more than three voices. This program employs the game paddles for the entering of notation and is a little easier to use than the MMI composer.
3. The Music Construction Set, from Electronic Arts,[8] is a popular program

[5]Electronic Courseware Systems, 309 Windsor Rd., Champaign, IL 61820 (217-359-7099).
[6]Electric Duet. Apple. Insoft, 1982.
[7]ALF Products, Inc., 1315 Nelson St. #F, Denver, CO 80215 (800-321-4668; 303-234-0871).
[8]The Music Construction Set. Apple. San Mateo, CA: Electronic Arts, 1982.

for the novice as well as advanced user. This program must be used with the Mockingboard synthesizer board if more than one part is desired. A joystick is also required.

Games. One of the truly novel and enjoyable areas of computer-assisted instruction is music computer games. These programs are designed to be fun while reinforcing or teaching a musical concept. Micro Music offers Arnold, a melodic diction game. Another company, Notable Software, specializes in game formats with its Note Trespassing, a note-naming game, and Musical Match-Up, a chord-matching game.[9] The University of Akron series (Wenger) also offers interesting games for teaching rhythm and naming musical symbols. These programs are a welcome addition to the music software library.

Music Performance and Advanced Applications. All of the above programs have one thing in common: there is no piano keyboard. However, several companies have developed piano keyboard systems for the Apple microcomputer: the Soundchaser, from Wenger, is one example. It uses a Mountain computer synthesizer board to hook to the Apple and is advanced enough to be used in live performances and for intricate recordings of up to 16 tracks. The system also offers music education software, which has the ability to transcribe music on a printer, and much more. The system may cost as much as $2,000 for the keyboard, synthesizer board, and operating software.

Art

For the creative child who has been drawing, cutting, folding, painting, and building models from clay, the need for assistance in producing art works may not be as necessary as for other children. For the child who does not feel as comfortable with the tools of the artist, the microcomputer screen and peripherals may encourage art projects which would otherwise be rejected.

Most of the art programs available for microcomputers are drawing and animation utilities. Unlike music, where the majority of programs are tutorials and drills, almost all the art programs are geared toward the creation of electronic art.

A peripheral that enhances the creation of computer graphics is the Koala Pad.[10] It plugs directly into the game port in the microcomputer and allows the user to draw intricate images, using the Micro Illustrator software which comes with the pad. The pad lists for just over $100 and is available for the Apple, Commodore,

---

[9]Notable Software, P.O. Box 1556 Dept. EM, Philadelphia, PA 19105.
[10]Koala Pad and Micro Illustrator. Santa Clara, Calif.: Koala Technologies Corp. Available from most computer dealers.

and IBM PC microcomputers. This is an excellent, inexpensive way to get involved with computer graphics. The Micro Illustrator software is amazingly well written and extremely easy for students to understand and use, in a matter of minutes. Overall, it is an excellent art tool for ages 7 through adult.

Another, more professional graphics peripheral is the Apple Graphics Tablet.[11] The list price of the tablet is approximately $700, including operating software. It can also be used with a number of other software packages. Because it is a delicate piece of equipment and should be used with care, it is best used by secondary school students. Many professional artists use the Apple Tablet in a wide variety of applications.

Light pens are also used to create computer graphics. With a light pen, one merely draws on the screen and uses the computer screen to draw lines and indicate areas for color fill. Joysticks used in many game programs are also used in a number of graphics software programs for drawing. The "mouse" is useful in both drawing and program operation. Light pens, "mice," and joysticks are available for many microcomputers and cost from $50 to $300. Purchasers are advised to check the software packages carefully to find out exactly what peripherals are needed with the computer. Occasionally, a package will be totally keyboard controlled, but such a package is generally much more difficult to operate to achieve the desired art effects.

Software companies have generally developed excellent software for computer art. Improvements are rapid and generally push the computer to the limit of its capability for resolution and color mixing. The art teacher may wish to choose the computer based solely on its capabilities for creating art. Computers such as the Amiga, the MacIntosh, and improved Atari machines boast graphics capabilities superior to those of the Apple and Commodore machines. In addition to the computers, a number of color printers are now on the market which can print the graphics onto paper in vibrant colors.

In selecting software, look for the packages which offer various kinds of art capabilities. With some programming background, students can learn to take the graphics created on various individual packages and pull them together onto a single disk or merge them with other programs. Such programming skills require a thorough knowledge of the DOS system of the computer, how each package records its graphics on disks, and how computer graphics are brought into RAM and displayed on the screen.

A few of the programs and types of software which are available currently are listed here as illustrative of the best. Software which will create individual pictures to be used in "slide shows" or as single pictures in other programs include the

---

[11]Apple Graphics Tablet. Apple Computer Corp. Available from any Apple Dealer.

popular Graphics Magician,[12] The Complete Graphics System,[13] and Dazzle Draw.[14] If students are interested in animation, Take 1,[15] with its many "actors" graphics disks, can be used to create entire cartoon or totally animated serious features. Lettering and other decorative graphic illustrations can be created with Fontrix[16] and the ever popular Print Shop.[17] Converting screen graphics to paper, either in black and white or in color, can be done using Triple Dump[18] or Paper Graphics.[19] These programs are called screen dumps because they take whatever picture can be captured on the screen and print it on paper.

Summary

Music and art present some of the most exciting possibilities for the use of microcomputers in education. There are, of course, the usual vocabulary or identification drill-and-practice programs and tutorial applications, but in the area of creative expression, microcomputers are providing many new, unique experiences.

The specific applications mentioned in this chapter are merely indicative of probes into a new world. Music applications include drill and practice to teach music theory and using the microcomputer as a music editor (a music processor similar to the word processor). Music synthesizers and microcomputers combine easily to become a new performance medium. Microcomputer programming, with music applications, is now appearing.

Art applications center on creation of a new form of expression known as *computer graphics*. Applications range from assistance in drawing to powerful tools to manipulate computer images. The exciting fact about artistic and music expression with the microcomputer is that excellent programs are available for a wide variety of microcomputers commonly used in schools.

The school library media specialist should work with art and music teachers to see that they are aware of the wide range of creative applications. These teachers should be able to help adopt the best of them. Special-equipment configurations may mean that certain microcomputers are dedicated to certain applications exclusively. These should be located in areas to which art and music teachers and their students have easy access.

---

[12]Graphics Magician. Apple, Atari, IBM. Geneva, Ill.: Penguin Software, 1983.

[13]The Complete Graphics System. Apple, Commodore, Atari, IBM. Geneva, Ill.: Penguin Software, 1983.

[14]Dazzle Draw. Apple. San Rafael, Calif.: Broderbund, 1984.

[15]Take 1. Apple. Grand Rapids, Mich.: Baudville, 1984.

[16]Fontrix. Apple. Denver, Colo.: Data Transforms, 1983. (The package has a number of additional font disks.)

[17]The Print Shop. San Rafael, Calif.: Broderbund, 1983. (Several picture disks and companion programs are available in addition to the original program.)

[18]Triple Dump. Apple. San Diego, Calif.: Beagle Bros. Micro Software, 1984.

[19]Paper Graphics. Apple, Commodore, Atari, IBM. Geneva, Ill.: Penguin Software, 1983.

Working with Social Studies Teachers

Fran Thompson

A number of exciting microcomputer applications are available in the area of social studies. These include a number of drill-and-practice, simulation, and tutorial-type software programs. The challenge for the teacher in social studies is to integrate the microcomputer as one of a variety of learning experiences. This challenges the school library media specialist to become a true instructional developer, that is, a person who facilitates instructional planning.

The following case study is an excellent illustration of the leadership of a school library media specialist, not only in curriculum planning with the teacher but also in skillful integration of a *wide variety* of media, including microcomputer software, into the learning environment. The result is an exciting and unforgettable experience for students and teachers.

Project CENT

Consumer Economics and New Technology, Project CENT, was a Title IVC program for two years in the Lafayette School Corporation. Its purpose was to integrate consumer education concepts into the curriculum via the integration of microcomputer programs and interfacing of microcomputers with video recordings and filmstrips. A team within each of the participating schools, consisting of a library media specialist and a classroom teacher, developed and used at least one economic education unit incorporating decision making and problem solving.

At Miami Elementary School in Lafayette, Indiana, the library media specialist and a fourth grade teacher developed the Project CENT unit on ''Economics and Energy.'' This project was selected because of the timeliness of energy conservation.

A section on energy resources is given in the social studies textbook which introduces the student to various kinds of energy and energy resources present in today's world.[1] This section normally covered problems associated with energy consumption, but it was expanded to incorporate and emphasize some basic economic concepts.

A two-week unit was planned, one week on energy and the other on economics, but flexibility was built in so that it could be lengthened and expanded as necessary. A little over three weeks was spent on the actual units, but the entire project evolved into one that spans the entire year. It incorporated many other disciplines: art, language arts, social studies, economics, media production, music, spelling, and computer literacy.

The teacher and library media specialist began the instructional planning and developing lesson plans during the summer, before the opening of school. The class consisted of 31 children, covering a wide spectrum of abilities. The teaching objectives, written jointly, were:

1. Students will have knowledge of the types of energy resources in today's world and where they come from.
2. Students will understand something of the amount of energy resources consumed and what alternatives will be available in the future.
3. Students will learn decision-making as they understand that, as energy resources dwindle or prices become too high, they will have to make choices.
4. Students will understand the concept of opportunity cost.
5. Students will understand the meaning of supply and demand.
6. Students will be able to relate the terms supply and demand to the energy market.
7. Students will be able to use the computer for learning.
8. Students will be introduced to simple computer programming and computer graphics so that they can use this knowledge to assist in developing an interactive filmstrip/computer program.

A student workbook was compiled and included a list of energy words (*oil, fossil fuels, natural gas, nuclear power, geothermal energy, wind power, thermometer, coal, generator, conserve, O.P.E.C.*) and an economic vocabulary (*price, consumer, surplus, supply, demand, scarcity, choice, opportunity cost*) for the students to explore and understand. Each pupil had a workbook into which the definitions of these words were written as their meanings were learned. Computer-created crossword puzzles[2] and word searches[3] were included to reinforce recognition and meaning of the words. There were maps, graphs, and activity sheets on energy and economics. The cover of the student workbook was created by using the Versawriter,[4] a drawing board and software system that enables

[1]David King, Jay L. Weisman, and Ronald Wheeler, *Environments* (Cincinnati: American Book, 1979).
[2]Crossword Magic. Apple. (Sunnyvale, Calif.: L & S Computerware, 1981).
[3]Elementary Volume 2. Apple. (St. Paul: MECC, 1981).
[4]Versawriter. Apple. (Newbury Park, Calif.: Versa Computing, 1980).

the user to produce computer graphics. The culmination was to be a student-produced filmstrip/tape which would be interfaced with the microcomputer. The energy unit was introduced with a filmstrip, *Energy in the Earth*,[5] which described the various energy resources and how they are used. A discussion followed. Students were then assigned energy words from the student workbook which they were to look up and write definitions. An Apple microcomputer was placed in the classroom and a computer program was created so that the students could match energy words and their definitions.[6] Vocabulary words were placed on another microcomputer program to permit the children to practice spelling.[7] These words were also included on the weekly classroom spelling test as bonus words.

Classroom Activities

In the classroom, the teacher discussed notetaking, outlining, and reporting. The class was divided into groups of three or four students, and each group was assigned a topic on energy to learn about and, subsequently, make a report. These topics included nuclear power, fossil fuel, water power, wind power, alternative energy sources, and O.P.E.C. Each group had to prepare a 10-minute oral report to present in class. Research on these topics made use of the resources of the library media center. When the reports were given in class, all students took notes on them, following an outline prepared by the teacher, so that each pupil would have a more complete awareness of the kinds of energy and the problems inherent in the use of that energy.

A listening center was set up in the classroom so that children could have access to a variety of materials for their study. A movie, *Energy Seekers*,[8] was shown to the class. This film presents a survey of current efforts to find new energy sources.

The economic unit was introduced with the filmstrip *Economics and You*,[9] which introduces some important economic concepts. The listening center featured additional filmstrips on economics during the study. The school library media specialist prepared some games which were also in a study center. The class used the game, Wide World of Energy,[10] a multimedia kit which consisted of a

---

[5]"Energy in the Earth," in *This World of Energy* (Washington, D.C.: National Geographic Society, 1981). Filmstrip.

[6]Shell Games. Apple. (Cupertino, Calif.: Apple, Inc., 1979).

[7]Elementary Volume 2. Apple. (St. Paul: MECC, 1981).

[8]*Energy Seekers*. (Lawrence, Kan.: Centron Films, 1980). 16mm, 11½ min.

[9]*Economics and You* (Bedford Hills, N.Y.: Teaching Resource Films, 1980).

[10]*The Wide World of Energy* (Burbank, Calif.: Walt Disney Educational Company, 1977). Multimedia kit.

filmstrip, study prints, and an energy game. A different economic concept was introduced each day. There were crossword puzzles and a word search (prepared by use of the microcomputer) on the economic words and their meanings. The students used microcomputer programs for matching words and definitions and for spelling economic words.

Simulation Games

The microcomputer program Lemonade[11] was also used. This software presents a simulated lemonade stand and the child has to make decisions on how many advertising signs to have, how much lemonade to make each day, and how much to charge per glass. The user wants to make as much money selling lemonade as possible.

Simulation games were used to introduce and reinforce concepts, and the media specialist brought two candy bars into the classroom as an example of a scarce resource. Discussion centered around the concepts of scarcity and the need to make a choice. The class had to decide who would get the candy bars. There were several rules: (1) the candy could not be divided and (2) there must be a majority decision on how the bars were to be distributed.

The class had a variety of suggestions: give them to those who were the quietest; to those with the best grades; to the ones who returned all their books to the library media center on time. And one child said, "Stop arguing. Just give them both to me!" The students were unable to reach a decision, so the teacher and the media specialist ate the candy!

The children then viewed the video cassette Choice,[12] from the Trade-Off series. In the video tape, Gordon has to make a choice about how he will use his time. Will he go to a ball game or the amusement park? The tape deals with the economic concepts *scarcity, choice,* and *opportunity cost.* On another day Malcolm Decides,[13] from the same series, was seen. Malcolm, an elementary-age child, receives a $25 gift certificate and has to decide what he will buy, using decision-making criteria.

Geologist's Dilemma,[14] another simulation game, demonstrated to the students that remaining fossil fuel reserves are unknown, and explained how difficult it is to find certain energy resources. In this activity, a handful of small colored beads

---

[11]Lemonade. Apple. (Cupertino, Calif.: Apple Computers, Inc., 1979).
[12]Choice. (Trade-Off Series). (Bloomington, Ind.: Agency for Instructional Television, 1979). Video cassette, 20 min.
[13]Malcolm Decides. (Trade-Off Series). (Bloomington, Ind.: Agency for Instructional Television, 1979). Video cassette, 10 min.
[14]Geologist's Dilemma, *Energy Trade-Offs in the Market Place* (Seattle: Washington State Council on Economic Education, 1980).

(each representing a type of fuel—e.g., black beads, coal; red beads, uranium; white beads, natural gas; yellow beads, oil; and cornmeal beads, solar power) was placed in an open container, then tossed into the air before the students arrived in the room. The class was divided into five companies—coal, uranium, natural gas, oil, and solar power—and given 1 minute to search for their company's energy. Each group counted their resources and was given 1 minute more for a second search. This activity reinforced the knowledge of both economic and energy concepts.

During the search, one group complained that they did not want to look for any more uranium (red beads) because they could not find many. They wanted to look for coal because more was available. This game proved to be both stimulating and enlightening.

Other Activities

Bulletin boards in the classroom centered around the energy and economic topics each week. The teacher used posters, charts, graphs, and pictures to reinforce the concepts.

A guest speaker, a metullurgical engineer from a local company, discussed how diminishing resources are "pushing" research for alternative energy. This particular company is producing windmills and pipes for wind and water power and compressed gas containers for cars. The pupils asked the speaker many questions, based on the energy and economic concepts they had studied.

The teacher found the Economic Action Pack[15] to be a very useful tool for teaching economic concepts. The accompanying booklet treats these concepts in a way fourth graders can comprehend. One page was used each day during the economic unit.

During the fall semester, the students were introduced to keyboarding on both the typewriter and the microcomputer. There was a typewriter and a typing manual in the classroom where they could practice. Typing Tutor II[16] and Master-Type[17] microcomputer programs were used to increase proficiency.

The teacher introduced the students to simple computer programming. She compiled a card index of computer activities for them to program. The children also used CAI programs in other disciplines.

After completion of the formal unit on economics and energy, production planning began. Miami School had just been renovated for fuel efficiency, so the

---

[15]Economic Action Pack (MacDonalds, 1981).
[16]Typing Tutor. Apple. (Bellevue, Wash.: MicroSoft, 1981).
[17]MasterType. Apple, Atari, Commodore, IBM. (Tarrytown, N.Y.: Scarborough, 1981).

teacher and the library media specialist capitalized on this for the filmstrip/tape program. Because of the students' interest in space, it was decided that the theme of the production would involve a space creature that would visit the school and the fourth graders would take the visitor on a tour of the school. The teacher also used an art class, in which each child designed a space creature. This creature had to be original—not similar to any movie or television characters.

After a creature had been designed by each child, there was a "brainstorming" session in which the children voted on which space creature to use in the filmstrip/tape. They named him Blurk. The session continued, with the students suggesting a general outline for the program. Blurk would come to earth in his spacecraft from the planet Huma, searching for "sootum" (which was the same as "fuel" on earth). The spacecraft would land on the school roof and the class would send representatives to find out what was happening. They would invite Blurk to tour the school with them so that they could point out ways Miami School is conserving energy. One afternoon, the assistant principal took the class on a tour of the building to point out just what had been done for energy conservation.

The class was divided into committees—script, storyboard, photography, audio taping, and microcomputer. With the library media specialist, the group wrote the script. They listed the economic and energy concepts they had studied and wove them into the writing. The storyboard committee divided the script for audio and visual matching. The teacher devoted several art classes to drawing and painting the background scenery. Sheets of white art paper, 12 by 18 inches, were used. Every child was assigned a background scenery picture to draw. Several children drew Blurk in many different positions and others sketched similar spaceships.

The principal characters in the filmstrip (children from the class) were photographed in a variety of positions, as required by the script. These positions included climbing, standing, pointing, and walking. The script also required that these photographs register numerous facial expressions indicating fright, laughter, conversation, and pleasure. The enlarged color prints, the pictures of the children, were cut out and mounted on the background drawings.

When the artwork and the pictures had been assembled, a committee photographed the pictures with a 35mm camera. The drawings were placed on a black cloth on the wall. Since there are two filmstrip frames for each 35mm frame, two of the 12- by 18-inch pictures were placed on the cloth in correct sequential order for each shot.

The microcomputer group helped the library media specialist write an interactive program for the microcomputer. One pupil used a graphic tablet to produce a computer picture of Blurk. Whenever the microcomputer was used for a question, Blurk would appear on the screen and say "Super!" for a correct response. The group used the Versawriter to make the title for the microcomputer program.

A Dukane Micromatic II, with an interface card attached, and the Apple microcomputer were used for this production project. This interactive program was entitled "The HUMAS Are Coming!" A certain number of frames of the filmstrip were shown. All the questions, formulated to relate to the students' environment and experience, required the user to make a decision. For example, one of the questions was, "The principal says we must do more to conserve energy than we are now. Which of the following can you do when you leave the classroom to help? (a) Turn off the lights; (b) Close the drapes; (c) Turn off the organ; (d) All of the above."

For the correct answer, Blurk, with the word "Super!" would appear on the screen. If the answer was wrong, the child would be given the right answer: "Would you really do just that? You could do all those things that were listed in the question." Then more frames would be shown and the students would be asked another question.

When the interactive filmstrip program was complete, the microcomputer and filmstrip were set up in the classroom and all the children evaluated themselves by using the program. A group of students demonstrated the program at a school open house (in the late spring) so that the parents and school patrons could view the work. The parents were excited and amazed at the accomplishments of their children.

Throughout the Lafayette School Corporation, one junior high school and five elementary schools were involved in Project CENT. Each team of library media specialist and teacher produced at least one interactive program. Teams concentrated on different concepts of economic education and either produced their own videotape or filmstrip or used commercially produced materials which were interfaced with the microcomputer.

Software on economics for elementary use on the Apple microcomputer is limited. Hot Dog Stand, Travel Agent Contest, and Smart Shopper Marathon[18] are simulation games for math which may be used in conjunction with economics. The software program Lemonade, already mentioned, has application in an economics education context.

Summary

Project CENT was a coordinated effort by the library media specialist and the teacher to develop instruction that is educationally sound and incorporates the microcomputer, as well as other media, into instructional activities. "Joint planning" meant that the teacher conducted some of the unit activities, the library media specialist conducted others, and they "teamed" the remainder.

The excitement, motivation, and learning experience for the fourth grade stu-

---

[18]Survival Math. Apple. (Pleasantville, N.Y.: Sunburst, 1982).

dents at Miami School for Project CENT was evident in their enthusiasm throughout the year. Economic education was the subject matter covered by this project, but interactive video/filmstrip microcomputer programming has wider potential and can be used in any discipline and subject matter. The use of interactive video/filmstrip for classroom application is in its infancy, but should be expanded in the future.

At the present time, microcomputers are not likely to be used for complete units of instruction in the social studies curriculum. Experience shows that they are better used when integrated into *parts* of units. They provide an excellent change of pace, as well as review. Drill-and-practice programs, identifying states, allow students to learn the locations of states in relation to one another, the states' capitals, and the correct spelling of both, as well as abbreviations for the states. These programs are not timed, and permit students to learn and practice at their own rates.

A number of social studies simulation games can become pure recreation rather than instructive tools. The library media specialist should work carefully with teachers to assure that software packages are designated for curricular uses and do not become ''Friday afternoon recreation.''

In the social studies, even a minimum number of microcomputers can make a difference, if activities and software are chosen wisely. The school library media specialist can help teachers choose programs for an entire class, using large-screen projectors. Such integration lends itself to this area of the curriculum.

Microcomputers in Mathematics and Science

Judith F. Speedy

Initial use of the computer by science and mathematics teachers began, on a limited basis, during the late 1960s and early 1970s. Its use was limited for a number of reasons, such as cost, availability, and teacher expertise. When computers cost thousands of dollars, school districts did not purchase computers as instructional tools, nor was there a highly trained teaching staff clamoring for their use. Commercially produced instructional packages were not available. As a result, programming, most often in FORTRAN, was taught to a select group of students, usually the mentally gifted. These limited experiences involved programming the computer to solve mathematical problems.

Teaching Math

The federal grant program ESEA Amendment in the 1970s combined the former ESEA Title II with NDEA Title III. This change provided an opportunity to purchase equipment for schools and school library media centers. At that time, many projects included the purchase of small calculators for the math departments. The abacus now sat on the shelf with the battery-operated hand calculator. When the microcomputer was perfected, math teachers eagerly adopted this advanced calculating machine with programming capability, and interest in instructional computing was regenerated.

School districts began to purchase several microcomputers for classroom use. These microcomputers were often restricted for use in math, and were further designed for students in classes for the gifted and talented. When a wider use was planned, the most frequent configuration to emerge on the secondary level was the grouping of these microcomputers into a computer lab under the supervision of the mathematics department. If this was the case, the primary instructional use was and remains, however, the teaching of programming languages. Today, BASIC has replaced FORTRAN as the language of choice in the secondary schools while a knowledge of Pascal has recently been added to meet the requirements of the SAT testing program.

Elementary teachers with an interest in teaching math were often the first to adopt microcomputers in their schools. As a result, others often assumed that the use of microcomputers was limited to the math curriculum. Changing this attitude is no less difficult in elementary schools than it is in the high schools. At this time, placement of the microcomputers can be dictated by a variety of needs, such as a computerized testing area, a math drill center, or a laboratory where every student receives individual instruction from both microcomputers and teachers.

A look at the program offered by the Gateway School District in Monroeville, Pennsylvania, which has a large number of graduating seniors with a computer science background provides one picture of how programming can be integrated into the high school mathematics curriculum. Two courses in BASIC programming are offered to high school students who have completed Algebra I. These courses, entitled Computer Math I and Computer Math II, teach programming primarily for use in problem solving. That is, the microcomputer is used as a tool to do mathematical calculations.

In the first course, students learn flowcharting and how to write simple programs. The second course focuses on subroutines, matrices, string variables, and special functions. In both courses, students produce programs appropriate to their level of mathematical training. The classes are taught in one of two microcomputer labs, each equipped with twelve Radio Shack TRS-80 microcomputers, a line printer and a networker. This equipment does not leave the lab nor is it used by other mathematics classes, because of the popularity of the computer math courses.

Four TRS-80 microcomputers are also available for use in the junior high school mathematics department. At this time, there is no formal program offering at this level. Use depends entirely on teacher and student interest and is almost exclusively supplemental. The elementary program is not yet implemented.

Since secondary programs were the first to be supported, the elementary teachers often brought in their own microcomputers to use with students. The pattern of use that developed crossed disciplines so no claim by one subject area developed. When computers were added by the district to the elementary schools, they were added to the library media centers so all grade levels and subject areas could make use of the technology.

If one looks at the trend for use of the computer in mathematics, it is now possible to teach whole courses of instruction on the microcomputer. The software for these courses or in-depth drill packages is expensive, but it is being purchased by many school districts with Title I funds. A common scenario is for the elementary teacher to cover math in the traditional way and then students are given from 15 to 20 minutes with a computerized math package. Documented increase in skills is impressive, but the gains may be due to the increased time spent on mathematics rather than the technique used. Theoretically, schools adopting full computerized math packages should integrate them into the regular instruction in such a way that an equal amount of time or less is spent on mathematics than before. Adopting this extensive use of software may not replace any math teachers in the school, but it certainly changes their role from exposition to guidance. Library media specialists can help as these entire curriculums are evaluated. Does the interest of students hold up over time? What library media center activities can counterbalance the emphasis on machine tutelage? Under the traditional curriculum, many library media specialists had little or no contact with math teachers. Will this pattern continue as machines intervene?

In addition to lengthy tutorials or drill software, there is a type which is very valuable to the math teacher. A number of programs on the market are almost simulations, but they can be used by teachers to teach concepts. The teacher may type in an equation or some math function and then manipulate data in those equations while students watch the result. For example, the teacher or student may enter values into an equation, and the computer will plot the curve or slope on the screen. Hundreds of graphs of functions are instantly available and provide a new way to teach math concepts. One example is Computer Graphing Experiments,[1] which explores graphs of parabolas, elipses, quadratic functions, etc. A game format for function graphing is present in the program Golf Classic/Compubar.[2]

Another popular approach to mathematics is the use of Logo to study geometry, calculus, and the graphing of functions. It can be used for many purposes by children and young adults, among which are creativity, problem solving, and encouragement of higher level thinking skills. Library media specialists should encourage math teachers to use Logo for its math capabilities, perhaps in cooperation with other teachers who want to use the program.

Finally, a number of textbook companies are issuing computer software to accompany their math textbooks. These disks may provide management systems for math teachers, repeatable tests, and supplementary computer math activities. An example is Math Activities Courseware,[3] produced by Houghton Mifflin Company, which has received praise from reviewers.

---

[1]Computer Graphing Experiments. Apple. (Reading, Mass.: Addison-Wesley, 1983).
[2]Golf Classic/Compubar. Apple, Atari. (St. Louis, Mo.: Milliken Publishing Co., 1983).
[3]Math Activities Courseware. Apple, IBM. (Boston: Houghton Mifflin, 1984).

Teaching Science

Using the microcomputer in the science curriculum provides many interesting possibilities and challenges. Most of these opportunities lie in two major applications: simulation and computer-operated scientific equipment.

A growing number of scientific programs are available which simulate scientific phenomena in ways that no other media or school experience can. In ecology, there is Balance—Predator-Prey Simulation,[4] which allows manipulation of food supply, carrying capacity, environmental conditions, and external pressures on animals and plants. Operation Frog[5] simulates dissection without the smell and mess. It has an additional advantage, in that all parts must be put back in their proper location. The programs Pest[6] and Three Mile Island[7] allow the student to work with dangerous pesticides and atomic reactors safely.

Control of experiments is another important function for the microcomputer. Almost any microcomputer can be attached to experimental equipment to monitor temperature, light, humidity, movement, pressure, etc. However, the microcomputer will have to be available without interruption for the duration of the experiment.

Science departments will probably want to have a number of computers dedicated to work in experimentation in addition to those needed in computer laboratories for simulation, tutorials, and drills. Library media specialists will need to work closely with the science faculty to ensure that both the hardware and software needed are available. In addition, since there is a gap between simulation and the real world, library media specialists may be able to assist science teachers in creating the realism needed to get the maximum benefits from the computer simulations used.

Computer Inservice Training

The Gateway School District developed a philosophy and goals statement for integrating the microcomputer into the K–12 curriculum. As often happens, it was developed after most of the hardware had already been purchased. While the specifics of a computer literacy curriculum were being planned, the district began to offer inservice training to its staff in the form of two three-credit computer literacy

[4]Balance—Predator-Prey Simulation. Apple, TRS-80, IBM. (Lafayette, Ind.: Diversified Educational Enterprises, 1982).
[5]Operation Frog. Apple, Commodore. (New York: Scholastic, 1984).
[6]Pest. Apple. (St. Paul: MECC, 1982).
[7]Three Mile Island. Apple. (Baltimore, Md.: Muse Software, 1981).

courses taught by the district's math teachers. Most of the teachers have been trained on a voluntary basis and paid the course fees.

The training of staff by members of the mathematics faculty who have been teaching programming or computer science, rather than the library media specialist, is the current practice at Gateway. This may not be the best way to train teachers. Programming is very threatening to persons who are not interested in programming, and most teachers view the microcomputer as having a programming application for the math teacher. Having the course taught by the math department may reinforce this impression rather than allowing teachers to see other applications. All teachers need to realize that several functions and roles for microcomputers are special to every discipline. Training can first begin with common functions, but eventually, specialized uses must gain attention.

Microcomputers and the Curriculum in a Single School

Jerry Wicks

It is anticipated that most of the readers of this book will be library media special-ists in a single school building. This concluding chapter traces the history of the implementation of the microcomputer program in just such a setting, Glenbrook North High School, Glenbrook, Illinois. To understand how the library media center has taken a leadership role in that implementation, one must know some-thing of the school and the library media program.

Glenbrook North High School draws students from an affluent suburb of Chi-cago. The median income is $55,000 a year (1981) and a number of well-known corporations are based in the area. A high percentage of the 2,350 students go to college; therefore, the emphasis is on academics with a moderate, but distinctive, vocational program. Expectations for quality public schools are high, and parents pay substantial tax money to insure that the school has the resources needed.

There are five elementary school districts which feed students to Glenbrook North High School, and each of these schools has a library media center and a full-time professional library media specialist. All have microcomputers in their li-brary media centers. All students come to high school with a good knowledge of library services and skills. All schools have excellent administrative support.

A good working relationship exists between the schools and the public li-braries, all of which are members of the North Suburban Library System. Recip-rocal borrowing privileges and interlibrary loan privileges are available, and the general public may use the high school's instructional materials center.

The Glenbrook North instructional materials center is operated by 15 staff members, 5 of which are certified. In addition to a coordinator, there is an audio-visual director who handles graphics, repair, the video studio, and the film li-brary. One floor professional handles all the periodicals and nonprint media; the second floor professional handles all print materials and the reference collection;

and a fifth professional handles all the cataloging and technical processing. Each of the professional staff members is a teaching professional and has teaching responsibilities. The coordinator is responsible for budgeting procedures and each department has a part in planning the library media budget.

For the 1983–84 school year, the budget of $107,000 included money for the purchase of materials, equipment, repair, and travel. An additional $60,000 budget for computers included equipment, maintenance contracts, software purchases, travel, and inservice training. For such a large budget, the collection is relatively small, about 25,000 books. Theft was a major problem until a security system was installed. Now the book collection is beginning to grow, and the staff has weeded it heavily.

The library media program has considerable visibility in the school and tremendous support from administrators, parents, and teachers. This support was extremely important when microcomputers appeared on the scene.

The Adoption Phase

In 1969, the district established a committee to work with computers. That committee conducted a study of district needs and made three recommendations which have now been implemented. The first was to acquire a main-frame computer for use by the administration at the district level. The second was to acquire a Digital PDP 11/44 minicomputer with multiple terminals and one megabyte storage for instructional computing. The third was to acquire numerous microcomputers and create computer laboratories for computer-assisted instruction and other computer learning.

The coordinator of the instructional materials center was appointed coordinator of instructional computing. This appointment was made so that all departments would have an opportunity to use the equipment. The committee wanted a very broad based program for instructional computing and looked to the library media staff as instructional leaders. This was an important decision for the school and one which took considerable political clout. Relationships with subject departments had been developing over a number of years, and leadership in instruction had already been established.

The program began with eight Apple microcomputers—four in the instructional materials center and four in the math resource center. The latter machines are the responsibility of the Instructional Materials Center. The Apple was chosen because of its graphic capabilities, and Apples have been purchased since this initial selection.

The library media staff had to learn this new technology, and they did everything they could to become familiar with it. They attended workshops and inservice training sessions, and they talked to everyone who was knowledgeable. None of the staff has had professional training.

Current Operations

The state of Illinois has a consortium on computers which has given Glenbrook North High School access to Minnesota Educational Computing Consortium (MECC) materials and has provided purchasing power. The district also belongs to a local consortium called Micro Ideas which now serves over 70 schools. This organization provides consultant services, preview privileges, and inservice training classes.

Currently there are 43 microcomputers in the high school building in addition to the Digital PDP 11/40 minicomputer. Twelve of the microcomputers are in the instructional materials center, 13 Apple IIe's are in a microcomputer lab, and 15 Apple IIs are in another lab. The remaining are in departments and in a work station for faculty in the instructional materials center. Both labs are next to and are part of the instructional materials center. The computers in the labs are standalone systems now, but plans are to network them. There are two mini-labs where the minicomputer and its 23 terminals are located. The labs are supervised by a paraprofessional, who not only supervises the equipment but also assists with the instruction.

The laboratories are used for regular classes in microcomputers and are available to any subject department to bring entire classes by appointment. The regular classes are taught by the department staff and consist of life-long uses of microcomputers—such as adapting programs, checkbooks, shopping lists, and bookkeeping systems for the home. The theory is that as adults students will always be using microcomputers in everyday life to manage homes and to manage work in a place of employment. Staff do not teach computer literacy—the students come to high school with those skills. The instructional materials center staff teach instructional computing. The math and business departments have computer science classes which expand students' knowledge in these particular areas.

Subject Department Use

One of the earliest and most frequent users of microcomputers was the music department, where microcomputers have been used in the advanced placement program. Its uses also include tone determination, rhythm study, and some composition.

The English department uses the microcomputers with the English as a second language program, the reading program, vocabulary drill, grammar, and composition. The junior-senior literary magazine is produced on the computer.

Other departments have used the microcomputer in a wide variety of ways. The social studies department has used some simulation and has used the microcomputer to drill students for the constitution test. The foreign language department has used the microcomputer for drill and vocabulary; the Spanish advanced placement test drill is particularly helpful. The math department makes heavy use of the microcomputers for drill and for various types of problem solving.

The business department has a beginning data processing course, an accounting on microcomputers course, and a COBOL course. Word processing is taught on A. B. Dick word processors. The physical education department uses microcomputers for management such as weight training, individual progress charts, stress management, and nutrition. The home economics department uses the microcomputer for nutrition, foods, and child development classes.

The microcomputer is used for industrial education to analyze heat loss, plan solar homes, and help build an actual home which is sold each year. The physics and chemistry departments use the microcomputer for a number of experiments and simulations. Of the 197 teachers on the staff, 170 of them have had at least six hours of inservice training on the microcomputer.

In analyzing use of the microcomputer by type of software, drill is used by most of the departments, particularly for review. Creative uses lag because good software has not been found, but one program assists students in the creation of poetry. Simulation has been particularly successful in the science areas. Word processing is making an impact in a number of curricular areas.

The staff members have not done a great deal of program creation themselves, but a number of brilliant students have created programs which are of use to the school. Many of these students write management programs or use programs such as DB Master to create vocabulary programs and other reviews.

Challenges

A number of problems have surfaced for which plans are currently underway to solve. There is a need to have more original programming, as well as to have someone to help teachers adapt software to their particular needs. No adequate system for preview exists at this time. More microcomputers are needed, and on-line searching of databases for students has yet to be implemented.

Real problems exist with the present building. The electrical wiring problem is a major one, and the microcomputers have created a need for an additional amount of space.

The Future

Looking into the future of microcomputing at Glenbrook North High School is not an easy task. One thing is certain: the support of parents, the school board, and administrators has been marvelous. These groups have been forward thinking.

The instructional materials center philosophy is that every student should become aware of computer possibilities, but should not necessarily know how to program computers. Computers are and will be a way of life for everyone; computers are not a fad—they are or will be a part of everything that is done.

The staff at Glenbrook North High School instructional materials center suggests that every library media specialist should be looked on as a leader in the use of the new technology and have the skill to train others. It is important to build a background of influence and confidence in order to move into a leadership role as the new technologies challenge school administrators, their staffs, and their students.

About the Authors

Richard E. Chase has been High School Media Director, Red Wing High School, Red Wing, Minnesota, for the past 18 years. He has used the Apple microcomputer in his library media center for the past five years and creates his own management programs. An active member of the Minnesota Educational Media Organization (MEMO), he makes frequent presentations and has taught at Mankato State University.

Marvin Davis, Media Director, Heartland Area Education Agency Media Center, has an M.S. in chemistry from North Dakota State University and an M.S. and Ph.D. in media from Iowa State University, Ames. He has served as President of the National Association of Regional Media Centers and on the LSCA Advisory Committee for the Iowa State Library.

Jean Donham, District Library Media Coordinator, Iowa City Community Schools, is a graduate of the University of Maryland School of Library and Information Services, and has been a District Coordinator for four years.

Doris Epler, Director, School Library Media Services Division, Bureau of State Library, Pennsylvania Department of Education, has an Ed.D. degree from Temple University. She is Director of the LIN-TEL project (electronic mail and database searching) for schools, public libraries, and community colleges in the Commonwealth. She is also responsible for directing the statewide effort to provide microcomputer training for teachers and administrators. She has been a computer programming teacher at the Berks Vocational-Technical School in Leesport, Pennsylvania.

Roger Flynn, Associate Professor in the Interdisciplinary Department of Information Science at the University of Pittsburgh, has a B.S. in philosophy from Villanova University, a master's degree in computer science from the Illinois Institute of Technology, and a Ph.D. in information science from the University of Pittsburgh. A popular teacher, he recently received the Apple Award for outstanding teaching in the College of General Studies at the University of Pittsburgh.

John Griffiths has been a systems professional for more than twelve years. He has worked with business and industry and taught college courses on systems for five years. As Consultant with the Innovative Technology Project, University of Pittsburgh, he has spent over a year training school teachers, librarians, and administrators in all aspects of microcomputers in schools.

Arly Gunderman, Principal, Pike Lake School, New Brighton, Minnesota, holds a B.S. and M.S. from St. Cloud University, an Ed. Specialist from St. Thomas, and is currently working on an Ed.D. degree. Mr. Gunderman is a past president of the Minnesota Elementary Principals' Association.

Deborah Hetrick, Consultant with the Innovative Technology Project, School of Library and Information Science at the University of Pittsburgh, has eight years' experience as a counselor and trainer and has trained teachers, librarians, and school administrators in hands-on use and understanding of microcomputers.

Jane Klasing, Educational Media Director with the Broward County Schools, Ft. Lauderdale, Florida, holds a B.A. from the State University of New York at Albany and an M.A. from Columbia University. Her present expertise includes the use of microcomputers in media management and administration and the use of databases via a phone modem.

James LaSalle, Computer Science Teacher, Ambridge Area School District Junior High School, Ambridge, Pennsylvania School District, holds a B.S. in education from Duquesne University, with postgraduate courses from the University of Pittsburgh, Penn State University, and Geneva College. Mr. LaSalle has also been employed as a commercial electronic technician and computer programming consultant, specializing in microcomputers. He has had computer programs published in national computer journals.

Jacqueline Mancall, Associate Professor in the College of Information Studies, Drexel University, holds a B.A. from the University of Pennsylvania, an

M.S. and Ph.D. from Drexel University. She is the author of widely read articles and books. Her research and teaching interests include applications of microcomputer software in the analysis of library processes, assessments of resource use, and the extension of searching potential.

Judy G. Mizik, Director, Division of Library Services, Board of Public Education, Pittsburgh, Pennsylvania, holds a B.A., M.Ed., M.L.S., and a Certificate of Advanced Study from the University of Pittsburgh, where she is currently enrolled in the doctoral program. In her present position she is responsible for the management of the LIN-TEL sites in school libraries, the use of OCLC in the centralized processing center, and for administering the LOGO program which has been placed in elementary school library test sites.

Nancy Olson, Professor and Audiovisual Cataloger, Mankato State University, Mankato, Minnesota, is a recipient of the coveted Esther Piercy Award. She is currently an OCLC visiting scholar and is a consultant to a special project to organize the Fred Rogers television tapes in the Nesbitt Collection at the University of Pittsburgh. She holds a B.S. in chemical technology from Iowa State University, and both an M.S. in curriculum and instruction and a Specialist degree in media from Mankato State University. She has taught cataloging at Mankato State University and is past president of the Minnesota Library Association.

Judith B. Palmer, Media Specialist in North Allegheny High School, North Allegheny School District, Pittsburgh, holds an M.L.S. from the University of Pittsburgh, where she is currently a doctoral student. Ms. Palmer has been a consultant in evaluating regional service centers.

Thomas Rudolph is currently Music Director, Haverford Township Public School, Haverford, Pennsylvania.

Judith F. Speedy, Computer Science and Library Media Specialist at the Gateway High School in Monroeville, holds an M.L.S. degree from the University of Pittsburgh, where she is currently a doctoral student. She has conducted workshops that train teachers and school librarians on the application of the microcomputer in the library and in the classroom.

Christopher C. Swisher is currently Assistant Director, Computing Resource Center, University of Pennsylvania. He earned a B.A. in literature from West Chester State University and an M.S. from the College of Information Studies at Drexel University. He has conducted many workshops in all areas of microcomputer use. He is author of numerous articles on microcomputer use in the library/information center.

Fran Thompson, Media Specialist, Miami Elementary School, Lafayette School Corporation, Lafayette, Indiana, holds an A.B. from Meredith College in Raleigh, North Carolina, and an M.S. from Purdue University. She has conducted in-school workshops, worked with all children in a K–8 school, and taught more than 500 students computer skills. She has also taught gifted fifth graders BASIC programming. She uses the microcomputer for daily circulation in her media center and uses word processing for school notes, letters, and class papers. She is responsible for purchasing software for the school.

Jerry Wicks, Coordinator, Instructional Materials Services, Glenbrook North High School (Glenbrook, Illinois), holds an A.B. from Millikin University and both an M.Ed and an M.L.S. from the University of Illinois. He has been a junior high school teacher, a director of a public library, and a principal. He is very active in professional associations where he has served on numerous committees. He is now on the Board of Directors of the American Association of School Librarians.

The book's editors are **E. Blanche Woolls,** Professor, School of Library and Information Science at the University of Pittsburgh, and **David V. Loertscher,** Associate Professor at the University of Oklahoma in Norman. They both hold Ph.D. degrees from Indiana University. They have conducted microcomputer workshops in several states, as individuals and as a team.